HISTORIC DECISIONS
OF THE SUPREME COURT

CARL BRENT SWISHER

*Thomas P. Stran Professor of Political Science
The Johns Hopkins University*

AN ANVIL ORIGINAL

under the general editorship of

LOUIS L. SNYDER

D. VAN NOSTRAND COMPANY, INC.

PRINCETON, NEW JERSEY

TORONTO   LONDON

NEW YORK

To a Long Line of
Students of Constitutional Law

D. VAN NOSTRAND COMPANY, INC.
120 Alexander St., Princeton, New Jersey (*Principal
office*); 24 West 40 St., New York, N.Y.
D. VAN NOSTRAND COMPANY (Canada), LTD.
25 Hollinger Rd., Toronto 16, Canada
D. VAN NOSTRAND COMPANY, LTD.
358, Kensington High Street, London, W.14, England

Library of Congress Catalog Card No. 58-8610

PRINTED IN THE UNITED STATES OF AMERICA

PREFACE

The purpose of this book is to bring together in brief compass revealing excerpts from Supreme Court decisions which are so outstanding that they may properly be labeled as "historic."

For more than a century and a half, opinions of the Supreme Court of the United States have revealed the fundamental character and responded to the throb of vitality of the American social order. To the Court have come the major issues of the scope of governmental power and the location of particular powers, whether in the national government or in the states and whether in one branch or another of the government. In its decisions are revealed the impact of industrialization upon our constitutional system and the effect also of transportation and communication changes which have brought the most distant parts of the world close to our door. Here it is that the phenomena of world change are translated into the language of constitutional law.

Because most Court opinions run to great length—a few, indeed, approximating the length of this entire book —ruthless cutting has been necessary in order to present even this limited number of cases. Concurring opinions have been omitted and only occasional brief excerpts from dissenting opinions have been presented to indicate the character of the opposition. For all the importance of dissenting and concurring opinions in the development of legal thought, even the names of differing justices have in general been omitted to leave room for fuller presentation of opinions on which at least majorities of the membership have agreed. It is hoped that these excerpts may not only illuminate the part played by the Supreme Court in American history but will also stir in some readers a desire to examine unabridged opinions in the more than three hundred fifty volumes of the official United States Reports.

CARL BRENT SWISHER

Baltimore, Maryland
January, 1958

TABLE OF CONTENTS

— 1 —

MARBURY v. MADISON

1 Cranch 137 (1803)

Marbury *v.* Madison *was the first of the outstanding opinions of Chief Justice Marshall. Marshall was the fourth Chief Justice to hold office but the first to make a vital impact on American constitutional law. The Marbury case involved a question whether the Supreme Court could strike down a federal statute which Congress had enacted believing it to be in harmony with the Constitution, but which the Court thought to be in conflict with the Constitution. The question involved relations between the Court and the other branches of the government, at a time when the Court was composed of Federalists and when Congress and the Executive were under Jeffersonian Republican control. Questions of party politics were mixed with constitutional questions about the scope of judicial power.*

Jeffersonians were opposed to interference by a Federalist judiciary. Yet here Marbury, whom President John Adams had appointed a justice of the peace, was asking the Supreme Court to issue a writ of mandamus to compel Secretary of State Madison to give Marbury the commission entitling him to hold that office. The Judiciary Act of 1789 authorized the Supreme Court to issue writs of mandamus to remedy wrongs of this kind, but the Constitution did not clearly authorize Congress to pass such an act. If a wrong was found to have been done, the Court would have to decide whether it would take action under a statute of doubtful constitutionality.

Putting the Jeffersonian administration definitely in

the wrong for refusing to issue the commission owed to Marbury as a result of action by former President Adams and the Senate, the Court found that Marbury was entitled to the commission; that principles of American law entitled him to redress; and that the writ of mandamus was the proper instrument of legal redress. It thus appeared that the Supreme Court would invite conflict with the Jefferson administration by ordering it to do what it did not want to do. But Chief Justice Marshall turned aside with the next step when he asked whether the Supreme Court was the proper tribunal to issue the writ of mandamus in such a case. He found that the Constitution narrowly circumscribed the original jurisdiction of the Supreme Court and did not include the power to issue the writ of mandamus. Should the Court obey the Constitution or the statute? The decision of the Court that it must obey the Constitution and not the unconstitutional statute entrenched in our constitutional system the practice of judicial review of acts of Congress.

↑   ↑   ↑

[Mr. Chief Justice Marshall] . . . . The question, whether an act, repugnant to the constitution, can become the law of the land, is a question deeply interesting to the United States; but, happily, not of an intricacy proportioned to its interest. It seems only necessary to recognize certain principles, supposed to have been long and well established, to decide it. That the people have an original right to establish, for their future government, such principles as, in their opinion shall most conduce to their happiness, is the basis on which the whole American fabric has been erected. The exercise of this original right is a very great exertion; nor can it, nor ought it, to be frequently repeated. The principles, therefore, so established, are deemed fundamental; and as the authority from which they proceed is supreme, and can seldom act, they are designed to be permanent.

This original and supreme will organizes the government, and assigns to different departments their respective powers. It may either stop here, or establish certain limits not to be transcended by those departments. The government of the United States is of the latter description. The powers of the legislature are defined and limited; and that those limits may not be mistaken, or forgotten, the constitution is written. To what purpose are powers limited, and to what purpose is that limitation committed to writing, if these limits may, at any time, be passed by those intended to be restrained? The distinction between a government with limited and unlimited powers is abolished, if those limits do not confine the persons on whom they are imposed, and if acts prohibited and acts allowed, are of equal obligation. It is a proposition too plain to be contested, that the constitution controls any legislative act repugnant to it; or that the legislature may alter the constitution by an ordinary act.

Between these alternatives, there is no middle ground. The constitution is either a superior paramount law, unchangeable by ordinary means, or it is on a level with ordinary legislative acts, and, like other acts, is alterable when the legislature shall please to alter it. If the former part of the alternative be true, then a legislative act, contrary to the constitution, is not law; if the latter part be true, then written constitutions are absurd attempts, on the part of the people, to limit a power, in its own nature, illimitable.

Certainly, all those who have framed written constitutions contemplate them as forming the fundamental and paramount law of the nation, and consequently, the theory of every such government must be, that an act of the legislature, repugnant to the constitution, is void. This theory is essentially attached to a written constitution, and is, consequently, to be considered, by this court, as one of the fundamental principles of our society. It is not, therefore, to be lost sight of, in the further consideration of this subject.

If an act of the legislature, repugnant to the constitution, is void, does it, notwithstanding its invalidity, bind the courts, and oblige them to give it effect? Or, in other words, though it be not law, does it constitute a rule as operative as if it was a law? This would be to overthrow, in fact, what was established in theory; and would seem, at first view, an absurdity too gross to be insisted on.

It shall, however, receive a more attentive consideration.

It is emphatically the province and duty of the judicial department to say what the law is. Those who apply the rule to particular cases must of necessity expound and interpret that rule. If two laws conflict with each other, the courts must decide on the operation of each.

So, if a law be in opposition to the constitution; if both the law and the constitution apply to a particular case, so that the court must either decide that case, conformable to the law, disregarding the constitution; or conformable to the constitution, disregarding the law; the court must determine which of these conflicting rules governs the case; this is of the very essence of judicial duty.

If then, the courts are to regard the constitution, and the constitution is superior to any ordinary act of the legislature, the constitution, and not such ordinary act, must govern the case to which they both apply.

Those, then, who controvert the principle that the constitution is to be considered, in court, as a paramount law, are reduced to the necessity of maintaining that courts must close their eyes on the constitution, and see only the law.

This doctrine would subvert the very foundation of all written constitutions. It would declare that an act which, according to the principles and theory of our government is entirely void, is yet, in practice, completely obligatory. It would declare that if the legislature shall do what is expressly forbidden, such act, notwithstanding the express prohibition, is in reality effectual. It would be giving to the legislature a practical and real omnipotence, with the same breath which professes to restrict their powers within narrow limits. It is prescribing limits, and declaring that those limits may be passed at pleasure.

That it thus reduces to nothing what we have deemed the greatest improvement on political institutions, a written constitution, would of itself be sufficient, in America, where written constitutions have been viewed with so much reverence, for rejecting the construction. But the peculiar expressions of the constitution of the

United States furnish additional arguments in favor of its rejection. The judicial power of the United States is extended to all cases arising under the constitution. Could it be the intention of those who gave this power, to say, that in using it the constitution should not be looked into? That a case arising under the constitution should be decided, without examining the instrument under which it arises? This is too extravagant to be maintained. In some cases, then, the constitution must be looked into by the judges. And if they can open it at all, what part of it are they forbidden to read or to obey?

There are many other parts of the constitution which serve to illustrate this subject. It is declared that "no tax or duty shall be laid on articles exported from any state." Suppose, a duty on the export of cotton, of tobacco, or of flour; and a suit instituted to recover it. Ought judgment to be rendered in such a case? ought the judges to close their eyes on the constitution, and only see the law?

The constitution declares "that no bill of attainder or *ex post facto* law shall be passed." If, however, such a bill should be passed, and a person should be prosecuted under it; must the court condemn to death those victims whom the constitution endeavors to preserve?

"No person," says the constitution, "shall be convicted of treason, unless on the testimony of two witnesses to the same overt act, or on confession in open court." Here, the language of the constitution is addressed especially to the courts. It prescribes, directly for them, a rule of evidence not to be departed from. If the legislature should change that rule, and declare one witness, or a confession out of court, sufficient for conviction, must the constitutional principle yield to the legislative act?

From these, and many other selections which might be made, it is apparent, that the framers of the constitution contemplated that instrument as a rule for the government of courts, as well as of the legislature. Why otherwise does it direct the judges to take an oath to support it? This oath certainly applies in an especial manner, to their conduct in their official character. How immoral to impose it on them, if they were to be used as the instruments, and the knowing instruments for violating what they swear to support!

The oath of office, too, imposed by the legislature, is completely demonstrative of the legislative opinion on this subject. It is in these words: "I do solemnly swear, that I will administer justice, without respect to persons, and do equal right to the poor and to the rich; and that I will faithfully and impartially discharge all the duties incumbent on me as ———, according to the best of my abilities and understanding, agreeable to the constitution and laws of the United States." Why does a judge swear to discharge his duties agreeably to the constitution of the United States, if that constitution forms no rule for his government? if it is closed upon him, and cannot be inspected by him? If such be the real state of things, this is worse than solemn mockery. To prescribe, or to take this oath, becomes equally a crime.

It is also not entirely unworthy of observation, that in declaring what shall be the supreme law of the land, the constitution itself is first mentioned; and not the laws of the United States, generally, but those only which shall be made in pursuance of the constitution, have that rank.

Thus, the particular phraseology of the constitution of the United States confirms and strengthens the principle, supposed to be essential to all written constitutions, that a law repugnant to the constitution is void; and that courts, as well as other departments, are bound by that instrument.

The rule must be discharged.

— 2 —

FLETCHER v. PECK

6 Cranch 87 (1810)

Fletcher *v.* Peck *performed great service to the nation in stabilizing the law of property rights particularly with respect to contracts for the purchase of land. Since the several states had but recently been carved out of virgin territory, the great body of property consisted of land rather than of industrial resources, and it was particularly important that land titles be firmly assured. Speculation in land ownership was comparable in kind to stock speculation in the twentieth century and widespread corruption prevailed, at times involving state legislatures. In this case a corrupted legislature in Georgia had sold a tremendous tract of land taken over from the Indians to a band of speculators for a small sum, and the tract had been broken up and resold at huge profits. A succeeding legislature repealed the grant but its power to disturb the newly acquired rights of "innocent third parties" was challenged. The Supreme Court was asked to pass on the initial right of the state legislature to dispose of the land and on the effect of the repealing statute. Dwelling upon the sanctity of the right of contract, the Supreme Court recognized the right of the state to make the initial sale, and held that the repealing act was unconstitutional as a violation of the contract clause and apparently also of natural rights principles. The decision did much to stabilize contract rights even as it permitted the speculators to enjoy the benefits of their misdeeds.*

[Mr. Chief Justice Marshall] . . . . The question, whether a law be void for its repugnancy to the constitution, is at all times a question of much delicacy, which ought seldom, if ever, to be decided in the affirmative in a doubtful case. The court, when impelled by duty to render such a judgment, would be unworthy of its station, could it be unmindful of the solemn obligations which that station imposes. But it is not on slight implication and vague conjecture that the legislature is to be pronounced to have transcended its powers, and its acts to be considered as void. The opposition between the constitution and the law should be such that the judge feels a clear and strong conviction of their incompatibility with each other. . . .

The lands in controversy vested absolutely in James Gunn and others, the original grantees, by the conveyance of the governor, made in pursuance of an act of assembly to which the legislature was fully competent. Being thus in full possession of the legal estate, they, for a legal consideration, conveyed portions of the land to those who were willing to purchase. If the original transaction was infected with fraud, these purchasers did not participate in it, and had no notice of it. They were innocent. Yet the legislature of Georgia has involved them in the fate of the first parties to the transaction, and, if the act be valid, has annihilated their rights also.

The legislature of Georgia was a party to this transaction; and for a party to pronounce its own deed invalid, whatever cause may be assigned for its invalidity, must be considered as a mere act of power which must find its vindication in a train of reasoning not often heard in courts of justice. . . .

The principle is this: that a legislature may, by its own act, devest the vested estate of any man whatever, for reasons which shall, by itself, be deemed sufficient. . . .

Is the power of the legislature competent to the annihilation of such title, and to a resumption of the property thus held? The principle asserted is, that one legislature is competent to repeal any act which a former legislature was competent to pass; and that one legislature cannot abridge the powers of a succeeding legislature. The correctness of this principle, so far as respects general legislation, can never be controverted. But, if an act be done under a law, a succeeding legislature cannot undo it. The past cannot be recalled by the most absolute power. Conveyances have been made, those conveyances have vested legal estates, and, if those estates may be seized by the sovereign authority, still, that they originally vested is a fact, and cannot cease to be a fact. When, then, a law is in its nature a contract, when absolute rights have vested under that contract, a repeal of the law cannot devest those rights; and the act of annulling them, if legitimate, is rendered so by a power applicable to the case of every individual in the community.

It may well be doubted, whether the nature of society and of government does not prescribe some limits to the legislative power; and if any be prescribed, where are they to be found, if the property of an individual, fairly and honestly acquired, may be seized without compensation? To the legislature, all legislative power is granted; but the question, whether the act of transferring the property of an individual to the public, be in the nature of the legislative power, is well worthy of serious reflection. It is the peculiar province of the legislature, to prescribe general rules for the government of society; the application of those rules to individuals in society would seem to be the duty of other departments. How far the power of giving the law may involve every other power, in cases where the constitution is silent, never has been, and perhaps never can be, definitely stated.

The validity of this rescinding act, then, might well be doubted, were Georgia a single sovereign power. But Georgia cannot be viewed as a single, unconnected, sovereign power, on whose legislature no other restrictions are imposed than may be found in its own constitution. She is a part of a large empire; she is a member of the American union; and that union has a constitution, the supremacy of which all acknowledge, and which imposes limits to the legislatures of the several states, which none claim a right to pass. The constitution of the United States declares that no state shall pass any bill of attainder, *ex post facto* law, or law impairing the obligation of contracts. . . .

Is a grant a contract? . . . A grant is a contract executed. . . .

It is, then, the unanimous opinion of the court, that,

in this case, the estate having passed into the hands of
a purchaser for a valuable consideration, without notice,
the state of Georgia was restrained, either by general
principles which are common to our free institutions,
or by the particular provisions of the Constitution of the
United States, from passing a law whereby the estate
of the plaintiff in the premises so purchased could be
constitutionally and legally impaired and rendered null
and void.. . .

[Mr. Justice Johnson]. . . . I do not hesitate to declare that a state does not possess the power of revoking
its own grants. But I do it on a general principle, on
the reason and nature of things: a principle which will
impose laws even on the Deity.

— 3 —

DARTMOUTH COLLEGE
v. WOODWARD

4 Wheaton 518 (1819)

*In the Dartmouth College case the Supreme Court,
perhaps in part inadvertently, took another long step
toward stabilization of the economic order. It held that
charters of private corporations (as distinguished from
public corporations such as towns and cities) were contracts, and that such charters were protected by the contract clause of the Constitution against impairment by
the states. The decision gave added stability to the rights
protected in private charters and made it possible for
the American people confidently to pool their economic
resources in private corporate enterprise instead of rely-
ing on government for the development of highways,
canals, railroads, and the various forms of industry.*

Immediately, however, the case involved not a business corporation but the charter of Dartmouth College which in 1769 had been granted by the English Crown to promote education in the wilds of New Hampshire, with the Christianizing and education of the Indians partly in mind. The college continued to thrive after New Hampshire became a state, but its president and trustees became embroiled in a political conflict between Jeffersonian Republicans and Federalists and in a denominational conflict between Presbyterians and Congregationalists. In 1816 the Republican-Presbyterian faction won control in the state legislature. The legislature proceeded to change the name of the college and transfer control to other hands. Representatives of the original college brought suit on the ground that the legislature had unconstitutionally impaired vested rights and violated the obligation of contract, with Daniel Webster making an impassioned argument on behalf of the college. The Court classified the college with private rather than with public corporations and held that New Hampshire could not impair its charter.

✓   ✓   ✓

[Mr. Chief Justice Marshall] . . . . This court can be insensible neither to the magnitude nor delicacy of this question. The validity of a legislative act is to be examined; and the opinion of the highest law tribunal of a State is to be revised—an opinion which carries with it intrinsic evidence of the diligence, of the ability, and the integrity, with which it was formed. On more than one occasion, this court has expressed the cautious circumspection with which it approaches the consideration of such questions; and has declared, that in no doubtful case, would it pronounce a legislative act to be contrary to the constitution. But the American people have said, in the constitution of the United States, that "no state shall pass any bill of attainder, *ex post facto* law, or law impairing the obligation of contracts." In the same instrument, they have also said, "that the judicial power shall also extend to all cases in law and equity arising under the constitution." On the judges of this court, then, is imposed the high and solemn duty of protecting, from even legislative violation, those contracts which the constitution of our country has placed beyond legislative control; and, however irksome the task may be, this is a duty from which we dare not shrink.

The title of the plaintiffs originates in a charter dated the 13th day of December, in the year 1769, incorporating twelve persons therein mentioned, by the name of "The Trustees of Dartmouth College," granting to them and their successors the usual corporate privileges and powers, and authorizing the trustees, who are to govern the college, to fill up all vacancies which may be created in their own body.

The defendant claims under three acts of the legislature of New Hampshire, the most material of which was passed on the 27th of June, 1816, and is entitled, "An act to amend the charter, and enlarge and improve the corporation of Dartmouth College." Among other alterations in the charter, this act increases the number of trustees to twenty-one, gives the appointment of the additional members to the executive of the state, and creates a board of overseers, with power to inspect and control the most important acts of the trustees. This board consists of twenty-five persons. The president of the senate, the speaker of the house of representatives of New Hampshire, and the governor and lieutenant-governor of Vermont, for the time being, are to be members *ex officio*. The board is to be completed by the governor and council of New Hampshire, who are also empowered to fill all vacancies which may occur. The acts of the 18th and 26th of December are supplemental to that of the 27th of June, and are primarily intended to carry that act into effect. The majority of the trustees of the college have refused to accept this amended charter, and have brought this suit for the corporate property, which is in possession of a person holding by virtue of the acts which have been stated.

It can require no argument to prove that the circumstances of this case constitute a contract. An application is made to the crown for a charter to incorporate a religious and literary institution. In the application, it is stated that large contributions have been made for the object, which will be conferred on the corporation as soon as it shall be created. The charter is granted, and on its faith the property is conveyed. Surely, in this transaction every ingredient of a complete and legitimate contract is to be found. The points for consideration are, 1. Is this contract protected by the constitution of the United States? 2. Is it impaired by the acts under which the defendant holds?

1. On the first point, it has been argued that the word "contract," in its broadest sense, would comprehend the political relations between the government and its citizens, would extend to offices held within a state, for state purposes, and to many of those laws concerning civil institutions, which must change with circumstances, and be modified by ordinary legislation; which deeply concern the public, and which, to preserve good government, the public judgment must control. That even marriage is a contract, and its obligations are affected by the laws respecting divorces. That the clause in the constitution, if construed in its greatest latitude, would prohibit these laws. Taken in its broad, unlimited sense the clause would be an unprofitable and vexatious interference with the internal concerns of a state, would unnecessarily and unwisely embarrass its legislation, and render immutable those civil institutions which are established for purposes of internal government, and which, to subserve those purposes, ought to vary with varying circumstances. That as the framers of the constitution could never have intended to insert in that instrument a provision so unnecessary, so mischievous, and so repugnant to its general spirit, the term "contract" must be understood in a more limited sense. That it must be understood as intended to guard against a power of at least doubtful utility, the abuse of which had been extensively felt; and to restrain the legislature in future from violating the right to property. That, anterior to the formation of the constitution, a course of legislation had prevailed in many, if not in all, of the states, which weakened the confidence of man in man, and embarrassed all transactions between individuals, by dispensing with a faithful performance of engagements. To correct this mischief, by restraining the power which produced it, the state legislatures were forbidden "to pass any law impairing the obligation of contracts," that is, of contracts respecting property, under which some individual could claim a right to something beneficial to

himself; and that, since the clause in the constitution must in construction receive some limitation, it may be confined, and ought to be confined, to cases of this description; to cases within the mischief it was intended to remedy. . . .

A corporation is an artificial being, invisible, intangible, and existing only in contemplation of law. Being the mere creature of law, it possesses only those properties which the charter of its creation confers upon it, either expressly or as incidental to its very existence. These are such as are supposed best calculated to effect the object for which it was created. Among the most important are immortality, and, if the expression may be allowed, individuality; properties, by which a perpetual succession of many persons are considered as the same, and may act as a single individual. They enable a corporation to manage its own affairs, and to hold property without the perplexing intricacies, the hazardous and endless necessity, of perpetual conveyances for the purpose of transmitting it from hand to hand. It is chiefly for the purpose of clothing bodies of men in succession with these qualities and capacities that corporations were invented and are in use. By these means, a perpetual succession of individuals are capable of acting for the promotion of the particular object, like one immortal being. . . .

From this review of the charter, it appears, that Dartmouth College is an eleemosynary institution, incorporated for the purpose of perpetuating the application of the bounty of the donors, to the specified objects of that bounty; that its trustees or governors were originally named by the founder, and invested with the power of perpetuating themselves; that they are not public officers, nor is it a civil institution, participating in the administration of government; but a charity school, or a seminary of education, incorporated for the preservation of its property, and the perpetual application of that property to the objects of its creation. . . .

This is plainly a contract to which the donors, the trustees, and the crown (to whose rights and obligations New Hampshire succeeds) were the original parties. It is a contract made on a valuable consideration. It is a contract for the security and disposition of property. It

is a contract, on the faith of which real and personal
estate has been conveyed to the corporation. It is, then,
a contract within the letter of the constitution, and within
its spirit also, unless the fact that the property is invested by the donors in trustees, for the promotion of
religion and education, for the benefit of persons who
are perpetually changing though the objects remain the
same shall create a particular exception, taking this case
out of the prohibition contained in the constitution. . . .

Almost all eleemosynary corporations, those which
are created for the promotion of religion, of charity or
of education, are of the same character. The law of this
case is the law of all. In every literary or charitable
institution, unless the objects of the bounty be themselves incorporated, the whole legal interest is in trustees,
and can be asserted only by them. The donors, or claim-
ants of the bounty, if they can appear in court at all,
can appear only to complain of the trustees. In all other
situations, they are identified with, and personated by,
the trustees; and their rights are to be defended and
maintained by them. Religion, charity and education are,
in the law of England, legatees or donees, capable of
receiving bequests or donations in this form. They appear in court, and claim or defend by the corporation.
Are they of so little estimation in the United States, that
contracts for their benefit must be excluded from the
protection of words which in their natural import include them? Or do such contracts so necessarily require
new modeling by the authority of the legislature that
the ordinary rules of construction must be disregarded
in order to leave them exposed to legislative alteration? . . .

If the insignificance of the object does not require that
we should exclude contracts respecting it from the protection of the constitution, neither, as we conceive, is the
policy of leaving them subject to legislative alteration
so apparent as to require a forced construction of that
instrument in order to effect it. These eleemosynary institutions do not fill the place which would otherwise
be occupied by government, but that which would otherwise remain vacant. They are complete acquisitions to
literature. They are donations to education; donations,
which any government must be disposed rather to en-

courage than to discountenance. It requires no very critical examination of the human mind to enable us to determine that one great inducement to these gifts is the conviction felt by the giver, that the disposition he makes of them is immutable. It is probable, that no man ever was, and that no man ever will be, the founder of a college, believing at the time that an act of incorporation constitutes no security for the institution; believing, that it is immediately to be deemed a public institution, whose funds are to be governed and applied, not by the will of the donor, but by the will of the legislature. All such gifts are made in the pleasing, perhaps delusive hope, that the charity will flow forever in the channel which the givers have marked out for it. If every man finds in his own bosom strong evidence of the universality of this sentiment, there can be but little reason to imagine that the framers of our constitution were strangers to it, and that, feeling the necessity and policy of giving permanence and security to contracts, of withdrawing them from the influence of legislative bodies, whose fluctuating policy and repeated interferences produced the most perplexing and injurious embarrassments, they still deemed it necessary to leave these contracts subject to those interferences. The motives for such an exception must be very powerful, to justify the construction which makes it. . . .

The opinion of the court, after mature deliberation, is, that this is a contract, the obligation of which cannot be impaired, without violating the constitution of the United States. This opinion appears to us to be equally supported by reason, and by the former decision of this court.

2. We next proceed to the inquiry, whether its obligation has been impaired by those acts of the legislature of New Hampshire, to which the special verdict refers. . . .

It results from this opinion, that the acts of the legislature of New Hampshire, which are stated in the special verdict found in this cause, are repugnant to the constitution of the United States; and that the judgment on this special verdict ought to have been for the plaintiffs. The judgment of the state court must, therefore, be reversed.

— 4 —

McCULLOCH v. MARYLAND

4 Wheaton 316 (1819)

The case of McCulloch *v.* Maryland *is noted both for its elaborate statement of the implied powers of the federal government and for its holding that a state may not tax an instrumentality of the federal government. Along with these issues of federalism the case involved an economic and political struggle between the Bank of the United States, chartered by Congress, and many smaller banks chartered by the several states. State banks at that time not only made loans as they do today, but issued as their own bank notes much of the paper money that served as hand-to-hand currency. Not being adequately restrained by state law, these banks often issued more notes than they were able to redeem on demand, with the result that the holders of their notes were in danger of losing their investment. The state bank notes circulated from person to person and from bank to bank, including the Bank of the United States. This institution often publicly identified state banks that had over extended their notes by refusing to accept the notes in the settlement of accounts, thereby embarrassing them and restraining their activities. In some states the local banks persuaded legislatures to enact laws restricting the activities of the branches which the national bank had established in a number of the states. The Maryland legislature in effect tried to tax the note issues of the Baltimore branch. When the branch failed to pay, suit was brought against the treasurer, McCulloch. Before the Supreme Court the national bank had to demonstrate its very right to exist, since the Constitution made no mention of any power of Congress to charter a bank or any other type of business corporation. Beyond that point, in order to win its case it had to demonstrate the unconstitutionality of the state tax on a federal instrumentality. The opinion by Chief Justice Marshall adds an important segment to the body of American constitutional law.*

✓   ✓   ✓

[Mr. Chief Justice Marshall] . . . . In the case now to be determined, the defendant, a sovereign state, denies the obligation of a law enacted by the legislature of the Union; and the plaintiff, on his part, contests the validity of an act which has been passed by the legislature of that state. The constitution of our country, in its most interesting and vital parts, is to be considered; the conflicting powers of the government of the Union and of its members, as marked in that constitution, are to be discussed; and an opinion given, which may essentially influence the great operations of the government. No tribunal can approach such a question without a deep sense of its importance, and of the awful responsibility involved in its decision. But it must be decided peacefully, or remain a source of hostile legislation, perhaps of hostility of a still more serious nature; and if it is to be so decided, by this tribunal alone can the decision be made. On the Supreme Court of the United States has the constitution of our country devolved this important duty.

The first question made in the cause is, has Congress power to incorporate a bank? . . .

This government is acknowledged by all to be one of enumerated powers. The principle, that it can exercise only the powers granted to it, would seem too apparent, to have required to be enforced by all those arguments which its enlightened friends, while it was depending before the people, found it necessary to urge; that principle is now universally admitted. But the question respecting the extent of the powers actually granted, is perpetually arising, and will probably continue to arise, as long as our system shall exist. In discussing these questions, the conflicting powers of the general and state governments must be brought into view, and the supremacy of their respective laws, when they are in opposition, must be settled.

If any one proposition could command the universal

assent of mankind, we might expect that it would be this —that the government of the Union, though limited in its powers, is supreme within its sphere of action. This would seem to result, necessarily, from its nature. It is the government of all; its powers are delegated by all; it represents all, and acts for all. Though any one state may be willing to control its operations, no state is willing to allow others to control them. The nation, on those subjects on which it can act, must necessarily bind its component parts. But this question is not left to mere reason: the people have, in express terms, decided it, by saying, "this constitution, and the laws of the United States, which shall be made in pursuance thereof," "shall be the supreme law of the land," and by requiring that the members of the state legislatures, and the officers of the executive and judicial departments of the states, shall take the oath of fidelity to it. The government of the United States, then, though limited in its powers, is supreme; and its laws, when made in pursuance of the constitution, form the supreme law of the land, "anything in the constitution or laws of any state, to the contrary notwithstanding."

Among the enumerated powers, we do not find that of establishing a bank or creating a corporation. But there is no phrase in the instrument which, like the articles of confederation, excludes incidental or implied powers; and which requires that everything granted shall be expressly and minutely described. Even the 10th amendment, which was framed for the purpose of quieting the excessive jealousies which had been excited, omits the word "expressly," and declares only that the powers "not delegated to the United States, nor prohibited to the states, are reserved to the states or to the people;" thus leaving the question, whether the particular power which may become the subject of contest, has been delegated to the one government, or prohibited to the other, to depend on a fair construction of the whole instrument. The men who drew and adopted this amendment had experienced the embarrassments resulting from the insertion of this word in the articles of confederation, and probably omitted it to avoid those embarrassments. A constitution, to contain an accurate detail of all the subdivisions of which its great powers will admit, and of all the means by which they may be carried into execution, would partake of the prolixity of a legal code, and could scarcely be embraced by the human mind. It would, probably, never be understood by the public. Its nature, therefore, requires that only its great outlines should be marked, its important objects designated, and the minor ingredients which compose those objects be deduced from the nature of the objects themselves. That this idea was entertained by the framers of the American constitution, is not only to be inferred from the nature of the instrument, but from the language. Why else were some of the limitations, found in the 9th section of the 1st article, introduced? It is also, in some degree, warranted, by their having omitted to use any restrictive term which might prevent its receiving a fair and just interpretation. In considering this question, then, we must never forget, that it is a constitution we are expounding.

Although, among the enumerated powers of government, we do not find the word "bank," or "incorporation," we find the great powers to lay and collect taxes; to borrow money; to regulate commerce; to declare and conduct war; and to raise and support armies and navies. The sword and the purse, all the external relations, and no inconsiderable portion of the industry of the nation, are intrusted to its government. It can never be pretended, that these vast powers draw after them others of inferior importance, merely because they are inferior. Such an idea can never be advanced. But it may with great reason be contended, that a government intrusted with such ample powers, on the due execution of which the happiness and prosperity of the nation so vitally depends, must also be intrusted with ample means for their execution. The power being given, it is the interest of the nation to facilitate its execution. It can never be their interest, and cannot be presumed to have been their intention, to clog and embarrass its execution, by withholding the most appropriate means. . . .

It is not denied, that the powers given to the government imply the ordinary means of execution. That, for example, of raising revenue, and applying it to national purposes, is admitted to imply the power of conveying money from place to place, as the exigencies of the nation may require, and of employing the usual means of conveyance. But it is denied, that the government has its choice of means, or, that it may employ the most convenient means, if, to employ them, it be necessary to erect a corporation. . . .

The power of creating a corporation, though appertaining to sovereignty, is not, like the power of making war, or levying taxes, or of regulating commerce, a great substantive and independent power, which cannot be implied as incidental to other powers, or used as a means of executing them. It is never the end for which other powers are exercised, but a means by which other objects are accomplished. No contributions are made to charity for the sake of an incorporation, but a corporation is created to administer the charity; no seminary of learning is instituted in order to be incorporated, but the corporate character is conferred to subserve the purposes of education. No city was ever built with the sole object of being incorporated, but is incorporated as affording the best means of being well governed. The power of creating a corporation is never used for its own sake, but for the purpose of effecting something else. No sufficient reason is, therefore, perceived, why it may not pass as incidental to those powers which are expressly given, if it be a direct mode of executing them.

But the constitution of the United States has not left the right of Congress to employ the necessary means, for the execution of powers conferred on the government, to general reasoning. To its enumeration of powers is added that of making "all laws which shall be necessary and proper, for carrying into execution the foregoing powers, and all other powers vested by this constitution, in the government of the United States, or in any department thereof." The counsel for the state of Maryland have urged various arguments to prove that this clause, though in terms a grant of power, is not so in effect; but is really restrictive of the general right, which might otherwise be implied, of selecting means for executing the enumerated powers. In support of this proposition, they have found it necessary to contend, that this clause was inserted for the purpose of conferring on Congress the power of making laws. That, without it, doubts might be entertained whether Congress could exercise its powers in the form of legislation.

But could this be the object for which it was inserted?
. . . That a legislature, endowed with legislative powers,
can legislate, is a proposition too self-evident to have
been questioned.

But the argument on which most reliance is placed is
drawn from the peculiar language of this clause. Congress is not empowered by it to make all laws, which
may have relation to the powers conferred on the government, but only such as may be "necessary and proper"
for carrying them into execution. The word "necessary"
is considered as controlling the whole sentence, and as
limiting the right to pass laws for the execution of the
granted powers to such as are indispensable, and without which the power would be nugatory. That it excludes
the choice of means, and leaves to Congress, in each
case, that only which is most direct and simple.

Is it true that this is the sense in which the word "necessary" is always used? Does it always import an absolute physical necessity, so strong that one thing, to which
another may be termed necessary, cannot exist without
that other? We think it does not. If reference be had to
its use, in the common affairs of the world, or in approved authors, we find that it frequently imports no
more than that one thing is convenient, or useful, or
essential to another. To employ the means necessary to
an end is generally understood as employing any means
calculated to produce the end, and not as being confined
to those single means without which the end would be
entirely unattainable. Such is the character of human
language, that no word conveys to the mind in all situations one single definite idea; and nothing is more common than to use words in a figurative sense. Almost all
compositions contain words which, taken in their rigor-
ous sense, would convey a meaning different from that
which is obviously intended. It is essential to just construction, that many words which import something excessive, should be understood in a more mitigated sense
—in that sense which common usage justifies. The word
"necessary" is of this description. It has not a fixed character, peculiar to itself. It admits of all degrees of comparison; and is often connected with words which in-

crease or diminish the impression the mind receives of the urgency it imports. A thing may be necessary, very necessary, absolutely or indispensably necessary. . . . This word, then, like others, is used in various senses; and, in its construction, the subject, the context, the intention of the person using them, are all to be taken into view.

Let this be done in the case under consideration. The subject is the execution of those great powers on which the welfare of a nation essentially depends. It must have been the intention of those who gave these powers to insure, as far as human prudence could insure, their beneficial execution. This could not be done by confining the choice of means to such narrow limits as not to leave it in the power of Congress to adopt any which might be appropriate and which were conducive to the end. This provision is made in a constitution intended to endure for ages to come, and consequently to be adapted to the various crises of human affairs. To have prescribed the means by which government should in all future time execute its powers would have been to change, entirely, the character of the instrument and give it the properties of a legal code. It would have been an unwise attempt to provide, by immutable rules, for exigencies which, if foreseen at all, must have been seen dimly, and which can be best provided for as they occur. To have declared, that the best means shall not be used, but those alone without which the power given would be nugatory, would have been to deprive the legislature of the capacity to avail itself of experience, to exercise its reason, and to accommodate its legislation to circumstances. If we apply this principle of construction to any of the powers of the government, we shall find it so pernicious in its operation that we shall be compelled to discard it. . . .

The result of the most careful and attentive considerations bestowed upon this clause is, that if it does not enlarge, it cannot be construed to restrain the powers of Congress, or to impair the right of the legislature to exercise its best judgment in the selection of measures to carry into execution the constitutional powers of the government. If no other motive for its insertion can be suggested, a sufficient one is found in the desire to remove all doubts respecting the right to legislate on that vast mass of incidental powers which must be involved in the constitution, if that instrument be not a splendid bauble.

We admit, as all must admit, that the powers of the government are limited, and that its limits are not to be transcended. But we think the sound construction of the constitution must allow to the national legislature that discretion, with respect to the means by which the powers it confers are to be carried into execution, which will enable that body to perform the high duties assigned to it, in the manner most beneficial to the people. Let the end be legitimate, let it be within the scope of the constitution, and all means which are not prohibited, but consist with the letter and spirit of the constitution, are constitutional.

That a corporation must be considered as a means not less usual, not of higher dignity, not more requiring a particular specification than other means, has been sufficiently proved. . . .

If a corporation may be employed indiscriminately with other means to carry into execution the powers of the government, no particular reason can be assigned for excluding the use of a bank if required for its fiscal operations. To use one, must be within the discretion of Congress, if it be an appropriate mode of executing the powers of government. That it is a convenient, a useful, and essential instrument in the prosecution of its fiscal operations is not now a subject of controversy. All those who have been concerned in the administration of our finances, have concurred in representing its importance and necessity; and so strongly have they been felt that statesmen of the first class, whose previous opinions against it had been confirmed by every circumstance which can fix the human judgment, have yielded those opinions to the exigencies of the nation. . . .

But were its necessity less apparent, none can deny its being an appropriate measure; and if it is, the degree of its necessity, as has been very justly observed, is to be discussed in another place. Should Congress, in the execution of its powers, adopt measures which are prohibited by the constitution; or should Congress, under the pretext of executing its powers, pass laws for the accomplishment of objects not intrusted to the government; it would become the painful duty of this tribunal, should a case requiring such decision come before it, to say that such an act was not the law of the land. But where the law is not prohibited, and is really calculated to effect any of the objects intrusted to the government, to undertake here to inquire into the degree of its necessity would be to pass the line which circumscribes the judicial department, and to tread on legislative ground. This court disclaims all pretensions to such a power. . . .

After the most deliberate consideration, it is the unanimous and decided opinion of this court that the act to incorporate the Bank of the United States is a law made in pursuance of the constitution, and is a part of the supreme law of the land. . . .

It being the opinion of the court, that the act incorporating the bank is constitutional; and that the power of establishing a branch in the state of Maryland might be properly exercised by the bank itself, we proceed to inquire—

2. Whether the state of Maryland may, without violating the constitution, tax that branch? That the power of taxation is one of vital importance; that it is retained by the states; that it is not abridged by the grant of a similar power to the government of the Union; that it is to be concurrently exercised by the two governments are truths which have never been denied. But such is the paramount character of the constitution that its capacity to withdraw any subject from the action of even this power, is admitted. The states are expressly forbidden to lay any duties on imports or exports, except what may be absolutely necessary for executing their inspection laws. If the obligation of this prohibition must be conceded—if it may restrain a state from the exercising of its taxing power on imports and exports—the same paramount character would seem to restrain, as it certainly may restrain, a state from such other exercise of this power, as is in its nature incompatible with, and repugnant to, the constitutional laws of the Union. A law, absolutely repugnant to another, as entirely repeals that

other as if express terms of repeal were used. . . .

The power of Congress to create, and of course, to continue, the bank, was the subject of the preceding part of this opinion; and is no longer to be considered as questionable. That the power of taxing it by the states may be exercised so as to destroy it, is too obvious to be denied. But taxation is said to be an absolute power, which acknowledges no other limits than those expressly prescribed in the constitution, and like sovereign power of every other description, is trusted to the discretion of those who use it. But the very terms of this argument admit that the sovereignty of the state, in the article of taxation itself, is subordinate to, and may be controlled by, the constitution of the United States. How far it has been controlled by that instrument must be a question of construction. In making this construction, no principle not declared can be admissible which would defeat the legitimate operations of a supreme government. It is of the very essence of supremacy to remove all obstacles to its action within its own sphere, and so to modify every power vested in subordinate governments as to exempt its own operations from their own influence. This effect need not be stated in terms. It is so involved in the declaration of supremacy, so necessarily implied in it, that the expression of it could not make it more certain. We must, therefore, keep it in view, while construing the constitution.

The argument on the part of the state of Maryland, is, not that the states may directly resist a law of Congress, but that they may exercise their acknowledged powers upon it, and that the constitution leaves them this right, in the confidence that they will not abuse it. . . .

The sovereignty of a state extends to everything which exists by its own authority, or is introduced by its permission; but does it extend to those means which are employed by Congress to carry into execution powers conferred on that body by the people of the United States? We think it demonstrable that it does not. Those powers are not given by the people of a single state. They are given by the people of the United States, to a government whose laws, made in pursuance of the constitution, are declared to be supreme. Consequently, the people of a single state cannot confer a sovereignty which will extend over them.

If we measure the power of taxation residing in a state, by the extent of sovereignty which the people of a single state possess, and can confer on its government, we have an intelligible standard, applicable to every case to which the power may be applied. We have a principle which leaves the power of taxing the people and property of a state unimpaired; which leaves to a state the command of all its resources, and which places beyond its reach, all those powers which are conferred by the people of the United States on the government of the Union, and all those means which are given for the purpose of carrying those powers into execution. We have a principle which is safe for the states, and safe for the Union. We are relieved, as we ought to be, from clashing sovereignty; from interfering powers; from a repugnancy between a right in one government to pull down what there is an acknowledged right in another to build up; from the incompatibility of a right in one government to destroy what there is a right in another to preserve. We are not driven to perplexing inquiry, so unfit for the judicial department, what degree of taxation is the legitimate use, and what degree may amount to the abuse of the power. The attempt to use it on the means employed by the government of the Union, in pursuance of the constitution, is itself an abuse, because it is the usurpation of a power which the people of a single state cannot give.

We find, then, on just theory, a total failure of this original right to tax the means employed by the government of the Union, for the execution of its powers. The right never existed, and the question whether it has been surrendered, cannot arise.

But, waiving this theory for the present, let us resume the inquiry, whether this power can be exercised by the respective states, consistently with a fair construction of the constitution? That the power to tax involves the power to destroy; that the power to destroy may defeat and render useless the power to create; that there is a plain repugnance in conferring on one government a power to control the constitutional measures of another, which other, with respect to those very measures, is declared to be supreme over that which exerts the control, are propositions not to be denied. But all inconsistencies are to be reconciled by the magic of the word confidence. Taxation, it is said, does not necessarily and unavoidably destroy. To carry it to the excess of destruction, would be an abuse, to presume which, would banish that confidence which is essential to all government.

But is this a case of confidence? Would the people of any one state trust those of another with a power to control the most insignificant operations of their state government? We know they would not. Why, then, should we suppose that the people of any one state should be willing to trust those of another with a power to control the operations of a government to which they have confided their most important and most valuable interests? In the legislature of the Union alone, are all represented. The legislature of the Union alone, therefore, can be trusted by the people with the power of controlling measures which concern all, in the confidence that it will not be abused. This, then, is not a case of confidence, and we must consider it as it really is.

If we apply the principle for which the state of Maryland contends, to the constitution generally, we shall find it capable of changing totally the character of that instrument. We shall find it capable of arresting all the measures of the government, and of prostrating it at the foot of the states. The American people have declared their constitution and the laws made in pursuance thereof, to be supreme; but this principle would transfer the supremacy, in fact, to the states. If the states may tax one instrument, employed by the government in the execution of its powers, they may tax any and every other instrument. They may tax the mail; they may tax the mint; they may tax patent rights; they may tax the papers of the custom-house; they may tax judicial process; they may tax all the means employed by the government, to an excess which would defeat all the ends of government. This was not intended by the American people. They did not design to make their government dependent on the states. . . .

— 5 —

GIBBONS v. OGDEN

9 Wheaton 1 (1824)

In peace time more federal authority over American enterprise is exercised through the power of Congress to regulate commerce with foreign nations and among the several states than on the basis of any other single constitutional provision. The Supreme Court first comprehensively discussed the commerce power in Gibbons v. Ogden in 1824, and then primarily in connection with the curbing of state power over interstate commerce. The broad interpretation of the federal commerce power there given, however, provided the basis for the sweeping exercise of federal power which began with the Interstate Commerce Act of 1887.

The case involved the constitutionality of a New York statute which gave to Robert Fulton and others a monopoly of the right to operate, on the waters of the state, boats powered by steam. The purpose of the statute was to give incentive to the development of the steamboat at a time when successful development seemed highly doubtful. In a few years, however, the steamboat revolutionized navigation and enriched the holders of the New York monopoly, who sought to extend their monopoly rights beyond the strictly internal waters of the state to waters connecting New York with other states. Other states retaliated with restrictive laws against out-of-state steamboats, threatening resumption of the chaos in interstate commerce which had existed before adoption of the Constitution. In this case Gibbons, who had no license from the New York monopoly but who did have a licence from the United States to operate in the coasting trade, was engaged in navigation between New York City and Elizabethtown, New Jersey. His right to do so was challenged by Ogden, who had a license from the New York monopoly. The task of the Court was to draw a line between the power of the state over its internal affairs and the power of the federal government to regulate interstate commerce.

✓   ✓   ✓

[Mr. Chief Justice Marshall] . . . . The appellant contends that this decree is erroneous, because the laws which purport to give the exclusive privilege it sustains, are repugnant to the constitution and the laws of the United States.

They are said to be repugnant: 1st. To that clause in the constitution which authorizes congress to regulate commerce. 2nd. To that which authorizes congress to promote the progress of science and useful arts.

The state of New York maintains the constitutionality of these laws; and their legislature, their council of revision, and their judges, have repeatedly concurred in this opinion. It is supported by great names—by names which have all the titles to consideration that virtue, intelligence and office can bestow. No tribunal can approach the decision of this question without feeling a just and real respect for that opinion which is sustained by such authority; but it is the province of this court, while it respects, not to bow to it implicitly; and the judges must exercise, in the examination of the subject, that understanding which Providence has bestowed upon them, with that independence which the people of the United States expect from this department of the government.

As preliminary to the very able discussions of the constitution, which we have heard from the bar, and as having some influence on its construction, reference has been made to the political situation of these states, anterior to its formation. It has been said, that they were sovereign, were completely independent, and were connected with each other only by a league. This is true. But when these allied sovereigns converted their league into a government, when they converted their congress of ambassadors, deputed to deliberate on their common concerns, and to recommend measures of general utility, into a legislature, empowered to enact laws on the most interesting subjects, the whole character in which the states appear underwent a change, the extent of which must be determined by a fair consideration of the instrument by which that change was effected.

This instrument contains an enumeration of powers expressly granted by the people to their government. It has been said that these powers ought to be construed strictly. But why ought they to be so construed? Is there one sentence in the constitution which gives countenance to this rule? In the last of the enumerated powers, that which grants, expressly, the means for carrying all others into execution, congress is authorized "to make all laws which shall be necessary and proper" for the purpose. But this limitation on the means which may be used, is not extended to the powers which are conferred; nor is there one sentence in the constitution which has been pointed out by the gentlemen of the bar, or which we have been able to discern, that prescribes this rule. We do not, therefore, think ourselves justified in adopting it. . . . We know of no rule for construing the extent of such powers, other than is given by the language of the instrument which confers them, taken in connection with the purposes for which they were conferred.

The words are: "Congress shall have power to regulate commerce with foreign nations, and among the several states, and with the Indian tribes." The subject to be regulated is commerce; and our constitution being, as was aptly said at the bar, one of enumeration, and not of definition, to ascertain the extent of the power, it becomes necessary to settle the meaning of the word. The counsel for the appellee would limit it to traffic, to buying and selling, or the interchange of commodities, and do not admit that it comprehends navigation. This would restrict a general term, applicable to many objects, to one of its significations. Commerce, undoubtedly, is traffic, but it is something more—it is intercourse. It describes the commercial intercourse between nations, and parts of nations, in all its branches, and is regulated by prescribing rules for carrying on that intercourse. The mind can scarcely conceive a system for regulating commerce between nations which shall exclude all laws concerning navigation, which shall be silent on the admission of the vessels of the one nation into the ports of the other, and be confined to prescribing rules for the conduct of individuals, in the actual employment of buying and selling or of barter.

If commerce does not include navigation, the government of the Union has no direct power over the subject, and can make no law prescribing what shall constitute American vessels, or requiring that they shall be navigated by American seamen. Yet this power has been exercised from the commencement of the government, has been exercised with the consent of all, and has been understood by all to be a commercial regulation. All America understands, and has uniformly understood, the word "commerce" to comprehend navigation. It was so understood, and must have been so understood, when the constitution was framed. The power over commerce, including navigation, was one of the primary objects for which the people of America adopted their government, and must have been contemplated in forming it. The convention must have used the word in that sense, because all have understood it in that sense; and the attempt to restrict it comes too late. . . .

The word used in the constitution, then, comprehends, and has been always understood to comprehend, navigation within its meaning; and a power to regulate navigation is as expressly granted, as if that term had been added to the word "commerce."

To what commerce does this power extend? The constitution informs us, to commerce "with foreign nations, and among the several states, and with the Indian tribes." It has, we believe, been universally admitted that these words comprehend every species of commercial intercourse between the United States and foreign nations. No sort of trade can be carried on between this country and any other, to which this power does not extend. It has been truly said, that commerce, as the word is used in the constitution, is a unit, every part of which is indicated by the term. . . .

But, in regulating commerce with foreign nations, the power of Congress does not stop at the jurisdictional lines of the several states. It would be a very useless power if it could not pass those lines. The commerce of the United States with foreign nations is that of the whole United States; every district has a right to participate in it. The deep streams which penetrate our country in every direction pass through the interior of almost every state in the Union, and furnish the means of exercising this right. If Congress has the power to regulate it, that power must be exercised whenever the subject exists. If it exists within the states, if a foreign voyage may commence or terminate at a port within a state, then the power of Congress may be exercised within a state.

This principle is, if possible, still more clear, when applied to commerce "among the several states." They either join each other, in which case they are separated by a mathematical line, or they are remote from each other, in which case other states lie between them. What is commerce "among" them; and how is it to be conducted? Can a trading expedition between two adjoining states commence and terminate outside of each? And if the trading intercourse be between two states remote from each other, must it not commence in one, terminate in the other, and probably pass through a third? Commerce among the states must, of necessity, be commerce with the states. In the regulation of trade with the Indian tribes, the action of the law, especially when the constitution was made, was chiefly within a state. The power of Congress, then, whatever it may be, must be exercised within the territorial jurisdiction of the several states. . . .

We are now arrived at the inquiry—what is this power? It is the power to regulate; that is, to prescribe the rule by which commerce is to be governed. This power, like all others vested in Congress, is complete in itself, may be exercised to its utmost extent, and acknowledges no limitations, other than are prescribed in the constitution. . . .

The power of Congress, then, comprehends navigation, within the limits of every state in the Union; so far as that navigation may be, in any manner, connected with "commerce with foreign nations, or among the several states, or with the Indian tribes." It may, of consequence, pass the jurisdictional line of New York, and act upon the very waters to which the prohibition now under consideration applies. . . .

In our complex system, presenting the rare and difficult scheme of one general government, whose action extends over the whole, but which possesses only certain enumerated powers; and of numerous state govern-

ments, which retain and exercise all powers not delegated to the Union, contests respecting power must arise.
Were it even otherwise, the measures taken by the respective governments to execute their acknowledged powers, would often be of the same description, and might,
sometimes, interfere. This, however, does not prove that
the one is exercising, or has a right to exercise, the
powers of the other. . . .

Since, however, in exercising the power of regulating
their own purely internal affairs, whether of trading or
police, the states may sometimes enact laws, the validity
of which depends on their interfering with, and being
contrary to, an act of Congress passed in pursuance of
the constitution, the court will enter upon the inquiry,
whether the laws of New York, as expounded by the
highest tribunal of that state, have, in their application
to this case, come into collision with an act of Congress, and deprived a citizen of a right to which that
act entitles him. Should this collision exist, it will be
immaterial, whether those laws were passed in virtue of
a concurrent power "to regulate commerce with foreign
nations and among the several states," or, in virtue of a
power to regulate their domestic trade and police. In
one case and the other, the acts of New York must
yield to the law of Congress; and the decision sustaining
the privilege they confer, against a right given by a law
of the Union, must be erroneous. . . .

Reversed and annulled.

— 6 —

CHARLES RIVER BRIDGE
v. WARREN BRIDGE

11 Peters 420 (1837)

*The advent of Chief Justice Roger B. Taney and of
other justices appointed by President Andrew Jackson*

marked not a sharp break with the past but a shift in trend. The new trend gave more emphasis to the powers of the states to govern their local affairs even when national affairs were incidentally involved. It was less "absolutist" where property rights were involved, giving more recognition to the power of government to police such rights and to limit them in the public interest.

The Charles River Bridge case marked such a limitation on the right of contract in corporate charters—a type of right which had been established by the Dartmouth College case. It limited the rights of a prosperous monopoly, in behalf of the power of a state to promote the economic welfare of its citizens. The rights involved dated back to 1650 when the Massachusetts legislature gave to Harvard College the right to maintain a ferry across the Charles River between Charlestown and Boston. In 1785 the legislature incorporated The Proprietors of the Charles River Bridge and authorized the company to build a bridge across the river at the ferry location, with compensation to Harvard College for the ferry rights. Tolls collected for crossing the bridge brought returns far beyond the cost of the bridge and the expectations of the legislature. The people grew tired of paying tribute, and in 1828 the legislature chartered another company to build the Warren Bridge a few rods distant from the first bridge. The Warren Bridge was to collect tolls until paid for and then become a free bridge. It quickly paid for itself and was opened to free transit, with the result that the public stopped paying tolls to cross the Charles River Bridge.

The case arose from the attempt of the owners of the old bridge to get an injunction to prevent the construction of the Warren Bridge. The Massachusetts court denied the injunction and the case went to the Supreme Court, where it was first argued before the Marshall Court but where its decision was delayed a number of years because the membership of the Court was incomplete and the participating members were divided in the case. The owners of the Charles River Bridge contended that their charter was intended fully to protect their rights as exclusive operators of a bridge in that area, and that the legislature, in authorizing construction of a competing bridge, unconstitutionally impaired the obli-

gation of the contract. The charter did not specify that the right was exclusive, but Daniel Webster and others who argued the case contended that charters should be interpreted broadly to give all rights that might reasonably be conferred, much after the fashion of interpreting constitutions, which, it was agreed, as a matter of principle should be interpreted broadly. Opposing counsel naturally emphasized the power of the state to legislate to promote the public welfare, and contended that corporate charters should be limited to the rights clearly and specifically given. The case was decided in favor of the Warren Bridge at the first term over which Chief Justice Taney presided.

↗   ↗   ↗

[Mr. Chief Justice Taney]. . . . It is very clear that in the form in which the case comes before us . . . the plaintiffs . . . must place themselves on the ground of contract, and cannot support themselves on the principle that the law devests vested rights. It is well settled by decisions of this court that a State law may be retrospective in its character, and may devest vested rights, and yet not violate the Constitution of the United States, unless it also impairs the obligation of a contract. . . .

Much has been said in the argument of the principles of construction by which this law is to be expounded, and what undertakings, on the part of the State, can be implied. The court think there can be no serious difficulty on that head. It is the grant of certain franchises by the public to a private corporation, and in a matter where the public interest is concerned. The rule of construction in such cases is well settled, both in England, and by the decisions of our own tribunals. In . . . *The Proprietors of the Stourbridge Canal v. Wheely et al.,* the court say, "the canal having been made under an act of Parliament, the rights of the plaintiffs are derived entirely from that act. This, like many other cases, is a bargain between a company of adventurers and the public, the terms of which are expressed in the statute; and the rule of construction in all such cases, is now fully established to be this—that any ambiguity in the terms of the contract, must operate against the adventurers, and in favor of the public, and the plaintiffs can claim nothing that is not clearly given by the act." . . .

Borrowing, as we have done, our system of jurisprudence from the English law; and having adopted, in every other case, civil and criminal, its rules for the construction of statutes; is there anything in our local situation, or in the nature of our political institutions, which should lead us to depart from the principle where corporations are concerned? . . . We think not. . . .

But we are not now left to determine, for the first time, the rules by which public grants are to be construed in this country. The subject has already been considered in this court, and the rule of construction, above stated, fully established. . . .

The object and end of all government is to promote the happiness and prosperity of the community by which it is established, and it can never be assumed that the government intended to diminish the power of accomplishing the end for which it was created. And in a country like ours, free, active and enterprising, continually advancing in numbers and wealth; new channels of communication are daily found necessary, both for travel and trade, and are essential to the comfort, convenience, and prosperity of the people. A State ought never to be presumed to surrender this power, because, like the taxing power, the whole community have an interest in preserving it undiminished. . . . No one will question that the interests of the great body of the people of the State, would, in this instance, be affected by the surrender of this great line of travel to a single corporation, with the right to exact toll, and exclude competition for seventy years. While the rights of private property are sacredly guarded, we must not forget that the community also have rights, and that the happiness and well being of every citizen depends on their faithful preservation. . . .

Adopting the rule of construction above stated as the settled one, we proceed to apply it to the charter of 1785 to the proprietors of the Charles River Bridge. This act of incorporation is in the usual form, and the privileges such as are commonly given to corporations of that kind. It confers on them the ordinary faculties of a corporation, for the purpose of building the bridge; and establishes certain rates of toll, which the company are authorized to take; this is the whole grant. There is no exclusive privilege given to them over the waters of Charles River, above or below their bridge; no right to erect another bridge themselves, nor to prevent other persons from erecting one, no engagement from the State, that another shall not be erected; and no undertaking not to sanction competition, nor to make improvements that may diminish the amount of its income. Upon all these subjects, the charter is silent; and nothing is said in it about a line of travel, so much insisted on in the argument, in which they are to have exclusive privileges. No words are used from which an intention to grant any of these rights can be inferred; if the plaintiff is entitled to them, it must be implied, simply, from the nature of the grant; and cannot be inferred, from the words by which the grant is made.

The relative position of the Warren Bridge has already been described. It does not interrupt the passage over the Charles River Bridge, nor make the way to it, or from it, less convenient. None of the faculties or franchises granted to that corporation have been revoked by the legislature; and its right to take the tolls granted by the charter remains unaltered. In short, all the franchises and rights of property enumerated in the charter, and there mentioned to have been granted to it, remain unimpaired. But its income is destroyed by the Warren Bridge; which, being free, draws off the passengers and property which would have gone over it, and renders their franchise of no value. This is the gist of the complaint. For it is not pretended that the erection of the Warren Bridge would have done them any injury, or in any degree affected their right of property, if it had not diminished the amount of their tolls. In order, then, to entitle themselves to relief, it is necessary to show that the legislature contracted not to do the act of which they complain; and that they impaired, or in other words, violated, that contract by the erection of the Warren Bridge.

The inquiry, then, is, does the charter contain such a contract on the part of the State? Is there any such stipulation to be found in that instrument? It must be admitted on all hands that there is none; no words that even relate to another bridge, or to the diminution of their tolls, or to the line of travel. If a contract on that subject can be gathered from the charter, it must be by implication; and cannot be found in the words used. Can such an agreement be implied? The rule of construction before stated is an answer to the question; in charters of this description no rights are taken from the public, or given to the corporation, beyond those which the words of the charter, by their natural and proper construction, purport to convey. . . .

Indeed, the practice and usage of almost every State in the Union, old enough to have commenced the work of internal improvements, is opposed to the doctrine contended for on the part of the plaintiffs in error. Turnpike roads have been made in succession, on the same line of travel; the later ones interfering materially with the profits of the first. These corporations have, in some instances, been utterly ruined by the introduction of newer and better modes of transportation and traveling. In some cases, railroads have rendered the turnpike roads on the same line of travel so entirely useless that the franchise of the turnpike corporation is not worth preserving. Yet in none of these cases have the corporations supposed that their privileges were invaded, or any contract violated on the part of the state. Amid the multitude of cases which have occurred, and have been daily occurring for the last forty or fifty years, this is the first instance in which such an implied contract has been contended for, and this court called upon to infer it, from an ordinary act of incorporation containing nothing more than the usual stipulation and provisions to be found in every such law. The absence of any such controversy, when there must have been so many occasions to give rise to it, proves that neither states, nor individuals, nor corporations, ever imagined that such a contract could be implied from such charters. It shows, that the men who voted for these laws never imagined that they were forming such a contract; and if we maintain that they have made it, we must create it by a legal fiction, in opposition to the truth of the fact, and the obvious intention of the party. We cannot deal thus with the rights reserved to the states; and by legal intendments and mere technical reasoning, take away from them any portion of that power over their own internal police and improvement, which is so necessary to their well-being and prosperity.

And what would be the fruits of this doctrine of implied contracts on the part of the states, and of property in a line of travel by a corporation, if it should now be sanctioned by this court? To what results would it lead us? If it is to be found in the charter to this bridge, the same process of reasoning must discover it, in the various acts which have been passed within the last forty years, for turnpike companies. And what is to be the extent of the privileges of exclusion on the different sides of the road? The counsel who have so ably argued this case have not attempted to define it by any certain boundaries. How far must the new improvement be distant from the old one? How near may you approach without invading its rights in the privileged line? If this court should establish the principles now contended for, what is to become of the numerous railroads established on the same line of travel with turnpike companies; and which have rendered the franchises of the turnpike corporations of no value? Let it once be understood that such charters carry with them these implied contracts, and give this unknown and undefined property in a line of traveling; and you will soon find the old turnpike corporations awakening from their sleep and calling upon this court to put down the improvements which have taken place. The millions of property which have been invested in railroads and canals, upon lines of travel which had been before occupied by turnpike corporations, will be put in jeopardy. We shall be thrown back to the improvements of the last century, and obliged to stand still, until the claims of the old turnpike corporations shall be satisfied; and they shall consent to permit these states to avail themselves of the lights of modern science, and to partake of the benefits of the improvements which are now adding to the wealth and prosperity, and the convenience and comfort, of every other part of the civilized world. Nor is this all. This court will find itself compelled to fix, by some arbitrary rule, the width of this new kind of property in a line of travel; for if such a right of property exists, we have no lights to guide us in marking out its extent, unless, indeed, we resort to the old feudal grants, and to the exclusive rights of ferries, by prescription, between towns; and are prepared to decide that when a turnpike road from one town to another had been made, no railroad or canal between these two points could afterwards be established. This court are not prepared to sanction principles which must lead to such results. . . .

The judgment of the supreme judicial court of the commonwealth of Massachusetts, dismissing the plaintiffs' bill, must therefore, be affirmed, with costs.

— 7 —

COOLEY v. BOARD OF WARDENS OF THE PORT OF PHILADELPHIA

12 Howard 299 (1852)

Although in Gibbons *v.* Ogden *(see Document No. 5) the Supreme Court interpreted broadly the power of Congress to regulate interstate and foreign commerce and held that a state could not enforce regulations in conflict with those of Congress, it left unanswered the question whether the states could regulate interstate or foreign commerce extending into its territory in the absence of federal regulation. The question, in other words, was whether the commerce power of Congress was exclusive or whether it could be shared with the states or could be exercised by the states prior to congressional action.*

The question arose in a number of cases during the Taney period, along with the question whether a state could, in the exercise of a primary power of its own such as one of its police powers, incidentally regulate interstate or foreign commerce. In New York *v.* Miln, *8 Peters 120 (1837), the Court upheld a New York statute requiring captains of ships to make reports on immigrants brought into the state, but the justices dif-*

fered over whether the commerce power was concurrent, whether the commerce had come to an end with the arrival of the ship, and whether the carrying of passengers, of human cargo, constituted commerce. In the so-called Passenger cases, 7 Howard 283 (1849), a sharply divided Court struck down state measures laying taxes on immigrant passengers. In the License cases, 5 Howard 504 (1847), the Court displayed like doctrinal confusion over the nature and extent of the power of states to prohibit the sale of liquor within their borders, especially when the liquor had been brought from other states and was sold in "original packages." The divided Court upheld the several state measures but with little clarification of principles.

The clarification came with the Cooley case, presented below. In 1789 Congress had declared its intention that navigation in the harbors and ports of the United States should continue to be regulated under the laws of the states. The movement of ships into and out of ports and harbors consisted in large part of interstate and foreign commerce, so that to the extent of the federal statute such commerce was left to state regulation. The case involved a challenge to the constitutionality of a Pennsylvania statute which provided for the regulation of pilotage in the port of Philadelphia. In deciding the case the Court drew a distinction between commerce which, though interstate or foreign, was essentially local and hence subject to local regulation, and commerce which was national in character and for which regulation required a national rule which only Congress could provide.

✓   ✓   ✓

[Mr. Justice Curtis] . . . . We think this particular regulation concerning half-pilotage fees is an appropriate part of a general system of regulations of this subject. Testing it by the practice of commercial states and countries legislating on this subject, we find it has usually been deemed necessary to make similar provisions. Numerous laws of this kind are cited in the learned argument of the counsel for the defendant in error; and their fitness, as part of a system of pilotage, in many places, may be inferred from their existence in so many different states and countries. . . .

It remains to consider the objection that it is repugnant to the third clause of the eighth section of the first article. "The Congress shall have power to regulate commerce with foreign nations and among the several states, and with the Indian tribes."

That the power to regulate commerce includes the regulation of navigation, we consider settled. And when we look to the nature of the service performed by pilots, to the relations which that service and its compensations bear to navigation between the several states, and between the ports of the United States and foreign countries, we are brought to the conclusion that the regulation of the qualifications of pilots, of the modes and times of offering and rendering their services, of the responsibilities which shall rest upon them, of the powers they shall possess, of the compensation they may demand, and of the penalties by which their rights and duties may be enforced, do constitute regulations of navigation, and consequently of commerce, within the just meaning of this clause of the Constitution. . . .

A majority of the court are of opinion that a regulation of pilots is a regulation of commerce, within the grant to Congress of the commercial power, contained in the third clause of the eighth section of the first article of the Constitution.

It becomes necessary, therefore, to consider whether this law of Pennsylvania, being a regulation of commerce, is valid.

The act of Congress of the 7th of August, 1789, sect. 4, is as follows:

"That all pilots in the bays, inlets, rivers, harbors, and ports of the United States shall continue to be regulated in conformity with the existing laws of the states, respectively, wherein such pilots may be, or with such laws as the states may respectively hereafter enact for the purpose, until further legislative provision shall be made by Congress." . . .

If the states were divested of the power to legislate on this subject by the grant of the commercial power to Congress, it is plain this act could not confer upon them power thus to legislate. If the Constitution excluded the States from making any law regulating commerce, certainly Congress cannot regrant, or in any manner reconvey to the states that power. And yet this act of 1789 gives its sanction only to laws enacted by the States. This necessarily implies a constitutional power to legislate; for only a rule created by the sovereign power of a state acting in its legislative capacity, can be deemed a law enacted by a state; and if the state has so limited its sovereign power that it no longer extends to a particular subject, manifestly it cannot, in any proper sense, be said to enact laws thereon. Entertaining these views, we are brought directly and unavoidably to the consideration of the question, whether the grant of the commercial power to Congress, did *per se* deprive the states of all power to regulate pilots. This question has never been decided by this court, nor, in our judgment, has any case depending upon all the considerations which must govern this one, come before this court. The grant of commercial power to Congress does not contain any terms which expressly exclude the states from exercising an authority over its subject-matter. If they are excluded, it must be because the nature of the power, thus granted to Congress, requires that a similar authority should not exist in the states. If it were conceded on the one side, that the nature of this power, like that to legislate for the District of Columbia, is absolutely and totally repugnant to the existence of similar power in the states, probably no one would deny that the grant of the power to Congress, as effectually and perfectly excludes the states from all future legislation on the subject, as if express words had been used to exclude them. And on the other hand, if it were admitted that the existence of this power in Congress, like the power of taxation, is compatible with the existence of a similar power in the states, then it would be in conformity with the contemporary exposition of the Constitution (Federalist, No. 32), and with the judicial construction, given from time to time by this court, after the most deliberate consideration, to hold that the mere grant of such a power to Congress, did not imply a prohibition on the states to exercise the same power; that it is not the mere existence of such a power, but its exercise by Congress, which may be incompatible with the exercise of the same power by the states, and that the states may legislate in the absence of congressional regulations. . . .

The diversities of opinion, therefore, which have existed on this subject, have arisen from the different views taken of the nature of this power. But when the nature of a power like this is spoken of, when it is said that the nature of the power requires that it should be exercised exclusively by Congress, it must be intended to refer to the subjects of that power, and to say they are of such a nature as to require exclusive legislation by Congress. Now the power to regulate commerce embraces a vast field, containing not only many but exceedingly various subjects, quite unlike in their nature; some imperatively demanding a single uniform rule, operating equally on the commerce of the United States in every port; and some, like the subject now in question, as imperatively demanding that diversity which alone can meet the local necessities of navigation.

Either absolutely to affirm or deny that the nature of this power requires exclusive legislation by Congress, is to lose sight of the nature of the subjects of this power, and to assert concerning all of them what is really applicable to a part. Whatever subjects of this power are in their nature national, or admit only of one uniform system or plan of regulation, may justly be said to be of such a nature as to require exclusive regulation by Congress. That this cannot be affirmed of laws for the regulation of pilots and pilotage is plain. The act of 1789 contains a clear and authoritative declaration by the first Congress, that the nature of this subject is such that until Congress should find it necessary to exert its power, it should be left to the legislation of the states; that it is local and not national; that it is likely to be the best provided for, not by one system or plan of regulation, but by as many as the legislative discretion of the several states should deem applicable to the local peculiarities of the ports within their limits.

Viewed in this light, so much of this act of 1789 as declares that pilots shall continue to be regulated "by such laws as the states may respectively hereafter enact for that purpose," instead of being held to be inoperative as an attempt to confer on the states a power to legislate, of which the Constitution had deprived them. is allowed an appropriate and important signification. It manifests the understanding of Congress, at the outset of the government, that the nature of this subject is not such as to require its exclusive legislation. The practice of the states, and of the national government, has been in conformity with this declaration, from the origin of the national government to this time; and the nature of the subject when examined is such as to leave no doubt of the superior fitness and propriety, not to say the absolute necessity, of different systems of regulation, drawn from local knowledge and experience and conformed to local wants. How, then, can we say that, by the mere grant of power to regulate commerce, the states are deprived of all the power to legislate on this subject, because from the nature of the power the legislation of Congress must be exclusive? This would be to affirm that the nature of the power, is, in this case, something different from the nature of the subject to which, in such case, the power extends, and that the nature of the power necessarily demands, in all cases, exclusive legislation by Congress, while the nature of one of the subjects of that power, not only does not require such exclusive legislation, but may be best provided for by many different systems enacted by the states, in conformity with the circumstances of the ports within their limits. In construing the instrument designed for the formation of a government, and in determining the extent of one of its important grants of power to legislate, we can make no such distinction between the nature of the power and the nature of the subject on which that power was intended practically to operate, nor consider the grant more extensive by affirming of the power, what is not true of its subject now in question.

It is the opinion of a majority of the court that the mere grant to Congress of the power to regulate commerce did not deprive the states of power to regulate pilots, and that although Congress has legislated on this subject, its legislation manifests an intention, with a single exception, not to regulate this subject, but to leave its regulation to the several states. To these precise questions, which are all we are called on to decide, this opinion must be understood to be confined. It does not extend to the question what other subjects, under the commercial power, are within the exclusive control of Congress, or may be regulated by the states in the absence of all congressional legislation; nor to the general question how far any regulation of a subject by Congress may be deemed to operate as an exclusion of all legislation by the states upon the same subject. We decide the precise questions before us, upon what we deem sound principles, applicable to this particular subject in the state in which the legislation of Congress has left it. We go no further. . . .

We are of opinion that this state law was enacted by virtue of a power residing in the state to legislate; that it is not in conflict with any law of Congress; that it does not interfere with any system which Congress has established by making regulations, or by intentionally leaving individuals to their own unrestricted action; that this law is therefore valid, and the judgment of the Supreme Court of Pennsylvania in each case must be affirmed.

— 8 —

DRED SCOTT v. SANDFORD

19 Howard 393 (1857)

For at least three decades before the Civil War the pattern of Supreme Court decisions was watched anxiously from both North and South for its implications for the issues of slavery. The commerce cases, for example, were eagerly followed. They involved questions whether the carrying of passengers was commerce. If it was commerce, then the carrying of slaves from state to state was interstate commerce, subject to federal control, while the power of the states over such transportation would be in some degree limited. Cases involving the return of fugitive slaves to their masters after escape into other states and of the punishment of persons who illegally aided slaves in escaping stirred deep emotions and bitter conflict. Admission of new states into the Union involved competitive struggles between northern and southern interests to preserve dominance. The North tried to keep slavery out of the territories which would become the new states and the South tried to implant its "peculiar institution" as widely as possible, denying that Congress had the constitutional power to prevent owners from taking their slave property into any territory of the United States.

The Dred Scott case is important in American history primarily because it was decided in such a way as to pass upon this question of constitutional power; because the North refused to accept the Supreme Court's limitation of constitutional power; and because it stirred still hotter the fires of sectional hatred. Dred Scott was at one time unquestionably a slave, held in the state of Missouri. His owner, an army surgeon, took Dred Scott with him to Illinois, where slavery was forbidden by statute. He later took him into the upper portion of the Louisiana Purchase, where slavery was forbidden by the act of Congress of 1820 known as the Missouri Compromise. Then he took him back to Missouri. Years later Dred Scott brought suit for his freedom, contending that he had become free through residence in free territory. Defeated in state courts, he brought suit in a local federal court on the basis of the constitutional provision giving jurisdiction in controversies "between citizens of different states," his owner at that time being a resident of New York.

When the case was argued in the Supreme Court, a majority of the justices at first agreed to decide it on the basis of an earlier decision holding merely that, whatever the legal rights of a slave when taken into free territory, when he returned to the state from whence he came his status was determined by local law—and by the law of Missouri, Dred Scott was a slave. But two justices insisted on writing dissenting opinions holding that a slave became free by virtue of residence in free territory and that Congress had the power to decree freedom in territory of the United States. The majority then decided to deal fully with the power of Congress, hoping to quiet public strife by holding that Congress had no constitutional power to deprive slave owners of their property by excluding slavery from United States territory. The following excerpts from the opinion by Chief Justice Taney reveal the strategy by which the court hoped to lessen slavery agitation, but which had the unintended effect of further inflaming public sentiment and increasing the threat of war. The Court held, among other things, that Congress had had no power to make Dred Scott a free man by virtue of his residence in free territory; that even if he had been free at some time while outside Missouri he was now a slave by virtue of Missouri laws; and that, in any event, as a Negro he could not be a citizen of the United States within the meaning of the Constitution and therefore could not sue for his freedom in a federal court.

✓   ✓   ✓

[Mr. Chief Justice Taney] . . . . The question is simply this: Can a negro, whose ancestors were imported into this country, and sold as slaves, become a member of the political community formed and brought into existence by the Constitution of the United States, and as such become entitled to all the rights, privileges and immunities, guaranteed by that instrument to the citizen? One of which rights is the privilege of suing in a court of the United States in the cases specified in the Constitution. . . . And this being the only matter in dispute on the pleadings, this court must be understood as speaking in this opinion of that class only, that is, of those persons who are the descendants of Africans who were imported into this country and sold as slaves. . . .

The words "people of the United States" and "citizens" are synonymous terms, and mean the same thing. They both describe the political body who, according to our republican institutions, form the sovereignty, and who hold the power and conduct the Government through their representatives. They are what we familiarly call the "sovereign people," and every citizen is one of this people, and a constituent member of this sovereignty.

The question before us is, whether the class of persons described in the plea in abatement compose a portion of this people, and are constituent members of this sovereignty? We think they are not, and that they are not included, and were not intended to be included, under the word "citizens" in the Constitution, and can therefore claim none of the rights and privileges which that instrument provides for and secures to citizens of the United States. On the contrary they were at that time considered as a subordinate and inferior class of beings, who had been subjugated by the dominant race, and whether emancipated or not, yet remained subject to their authority, and had no rights or privileges but such as those who held the power and the Government might choose to grant them. . . .

In discussing this question, we must not confound the rights of citizenship which a State may confer within its own limits, and the rights of citizenship as a member of the Union. It does not by any means follow, because he has all the rights and privileges of a citizen of a State, that he must be a citizen of the United States. He may have all the rights and privileges of the citizen of a State, and yet not be entitled to the rights and privileges of a citizen in any other State. For, previous to the adoption of the Constitution of the United States, every State had the undoubted right to confer on whomsoever it pleased the character of citizen, and to endow him with all his rights. But this character of course was confined to the boundaries of the State, and gave him no rights or privileges in other States beyond those secured to him by the laws of nations and the comity of States. Nor have the several States surrendered the power of conferring these rights and privileges by adopting the Constitution of the United States. . . .

It is very clear, therefore, that no State can, by any act or law of its own, passed since the adoption of the Constitution, introduce a new member into the political community created by the Constitution of the United States. It cannot make him a member of this community by making him a member of its own. And for the same reason it cannot introduce any person, or description of persons, who are not intended to be embraced in this new political family, which the Constitution brought into existence, but were intended to be excluded from it.

The question then arises, whether the provisions of the Constitution, in relation to the personal rights and privileges to which the citizen of a State should be entitled, embraced the negro African race, at that time in this country, or who might afterwards be imported, who had then or should afterwards be made free in any State; and to put it in the power of a single State to make him a citizen of the United States, and endow him with the full rights of citizenship in every other State without their consent? Does the Constitution of the United States act upon him whenever he shall be made free under the laws of a State, and raised there to the rank of a citizen, and immediately clothe him with all the privileges of a citizen in every State, and in its own courts?

The court think the affirmative of these propositions cannot be maintained. And if it cannot, the plaintiff in error could not be a citizen of the State of Missouri, within the meaning of the Constitution of the United States, and, consequently, was not entitled to sue in its courts.

It is true, every person, and every class and description of persons, who were at the time of the adoption of the Constitution recognized as citizens in the several States, became also citizens of this new political body; but none other; it was formed by them, and for them and their posterity, but for no one else. And the personal rights and privileges guaranteed to citizens of this new sovereignty were intended to embrace those only who were then members of the several State communities, or who should afterwards, by birthright or otherwise, become members, according to the provisions of the Constitution and the principles on which it was founded. It was the union of those who were at that time members of distinct and separate political communities into one political family, whose power, for certain specified purposes, was to extend over the whole territory of the United States. And it gave to each citizen rights and privileges outside of his State which he did not before possess, and placed him in every other State upon a perfect equality with its own citizens as to rights of person and rights of property; it made him a citizen of the United States. . . .

In the opinion of the court, the legislation and histories of the times, and the language used in the Declaration of Independence, show, that neither the class of persons who had been imported as slaves, nor their descendants, whether they had become free or not, were then acknowledged as a part of the people, nor intended to be included in the general words used in that memorable instrument. . . .

They had for more than a century before been regarded as beings of an inferior order, and altogether unfit to associate with the white race, either in social or political relations; and so far inferior, that they had no rights which the white man was bound to respect; and that the negro might justly and lawfully be reduced to slavery for his benefit. . . .

The legislation of the different colonies furnishes positive and indisputable proof of this fact. . . . The language of the Declaration of Independence is equally conclusive. . . . This state of public opinion had undergone no change when the Constitution was adopted, as is equally evident from its provisions and language. . . . But there are two clauses in the Constitution which point directly and specifically to the negro race as a separate class of persons, and show clearly that they were not regarded as a portion of the people or citizens of the Government then formed.

One of these clauses reserves to each of the thirteen States the right to import slaves until the year 1808, if it thinks proper. . . . And by the other provision the States pledge themselves to each other to maintain the right of property of the master, by delivering up to him any slave who may have escaped from his service, and be found within their respective territories. . . .

The legislation of the States therefore shows, in a manner not to be mistaken, the inferior and subject condition of that race at the time the Constitution was adopted, and long afterwards, throughout the thirteen States by which that instrument was framed; and it is hardly consistent with respect due to these States, to suppose that they regarded at that time, as fellow-citizens and members of the sovereignty, a class of beings whom they had thus stigmatized; whom, as we are bound, out of respect to the State sovereignties, to assume they had deemed it just and necessary thus to stigmatize, and upon whom they had impressed such deep and enduring marks of inferiority and degradation; or, that when they met in convention to form the Constitution, they looked upon them as a portion of their constituents, or designed to include them in the provisions so carefully inserted for the security and protection of the liberties and rights of their citizens. It cannot be supposed that they intended to secure to them rights, and privileges, and rank, in the new political body throughout the Union, which every one of them denied within the limits of its own dominion. More especially, it cannot be believed that the large slave-holding States regarded them as included in the word citizens, or would have consented to a Constitution which might compel them to receive them in that character from another State. . . .

The act of Congress [the Missouri Compromise], upon which the plaintiff relies, declares that slavery and involuntary servitude, except as a punishment for crime, shall be forever prohibited in all that part of the territory ceded by France, under the name of Louisiana, which lies north of thirty-six degrees thirty minutes north latitude, and not included within the limits of Missouri. And the difficulty which meets us at the threshold of this part of the inquiry is, whether Congress was authorized to pass this law, under any of the powers granted to it by the Constitution; for if the authority is not given by that instrument, it is the duty of this court to declare it void and inoperative, and incapable of conferring freedom upon any one who is held as a slave under the laws of any one of the States. . . .

It seems . . . to be supposed, that there is a difference between property in a slave and other property, and that different rules may be applied to it in expounding the Constitution of the United States. And the laws and usages of nations, and the writings of eminent jurists upon the relation of master and slave and their mutual rights and duties, and the powers which Governments may exercise over it, have been dwelt upon in the argument.

But in considering the question before us, it must be borne in mind that there is no law of nations standing between the people of the United States and their Government, and interfering with their relation to each other. The powers of the Government, and the rights of the citizens under it, are positive and practical regulations plainly written down. The people of the United States have delegated to it certain enumerated powers, and forbidden it to exercise others. It has no power over the person or property of a citizen but what the citizens of the United States have granted. And no laws or usages of other nations, or reasoning of statesmen or jurists upon the relations of master and slave, can enlarge the powers of the Government, or take from the citizens the rights they have reserved. And if the Constitution recognizes the right of property of the master in a slave, and makes no distinction between that description of property and other property owned by a citizen, no tribunal acting under the authority of the United States, whether it be legislative, executive, or judicial, has a right to draw such a distinction, or deny to it the benefit of the provisions and guarantees which have been provided for the protection of private property against encroachments of the Government. . . .

Upon these considerations, it is the opinion of the court that the act of Congress which prohibited a citizen from holding or owning property of this kind in the territory of the United States north of the line therein mentioned, is not warranted by the Constitution, and is therefore void; and that neither Dred Scott himself, nor any of his family, were made free by being carried into this territory; even if they had been carried there by the owner, with the intention of becoming a permanent resident. . . .

— 9 —

THE PRIZE CASES

2 Black 635 (1863)

When in April, 1861, the forces of the southern Confederacy began hostilities against the Union, President Lincoln started counter war measures without waiting for Congress to meet and declare war. Among other things he proclaimed a blockade of southern ports according to the rules of international law, and Union ships began to seize as prize the foreign ships which were caught running the blockade. The owners of some of these ships contested the legality of the seizure, contending that the conflict had the status only of an internal insurrection and not of a war, and that in the absence of a conflict between lawful belligerents or of a declaration of war by Congress the blockade could not be enforced. Great anxiety accompanied the argument of the cases before the Supreme Court because of the fear that the Court might hold that the blockade was illegal and thereby seriously embroil the United States with the governments whose ships had been seized. Fortunately a majority of the Court upheld the enforcement of the blockade from the date when it was proclaimed, and the remaining justices saw it as valid from the time when Congress enacted supporting legislation.

✦   ✦   ✦

[Mr. Justice Grier] . . . . Had the President a right to institute a blockade of ports in possession of persons in armed rebellion against the government, on the principles of international law, as known and acknowledged among civilized States? . . .

Neutrals have a right to challenge the existence of a blockade *de facto* and also the authority of the party exercising the right to institute it. They have a right to enter the ports of a friendly nation for the purposes of trade and commerce, but are bound to recognize the rights of a belligerent engaged in actual war, to use this mode of coercion, for the purpose of subduing the enemy.

That a blockade *de facto* actually existed, and was formally declared and notified by the President on the 27th and 30th of April, 1861, is an admitted fact in these cases.

That the President, as the Executive Chief of the Government and Commander-in-Chief of the Army and Navy, was the proper person to make such notification, has not been and cannot be disputed.

The right of prize and capture has its origin in the *jus belli,* and is governed and adjudged under the law of nations. To legitimate the capture of a neutral vessel or property on the high seas, a war must exist *de facto,* and the neutral must have a knowledge or notice of the intention of one of the parties belligerent to use this mode of coercion against a port, city, or territory, in possession of the other.

Let us enquire whether, at the time this blockade was instituted, a state of war existed which would justify a resort to these means of subduing the hostile force.

War has been well defined to be, "That state in which a nation prosecutes its right by force."

The parties belligerent in a public war are independent nations. But it is not necessary to constitute war, that both parties should be acknowledged as independent nations or sovereign States. A war may exist where one of the belligerents claims sovereign rights as against the other. . . . A civil war always begins by insurrection against the lawful authority of the Government. . . . As a civil war is never publicly proclaimed, *eo nomine,* against insurgents, its actual existence is a fact in our domestic history which the Court is bound to notice and to know. . . .

By the Constitution, Congress alone has the power to declare a national or foreign war. It cannot declare war against a State, or any number of States, by virtue of any clause in the Constitution. The Constitution confers on

the President the whole Executive power. He is bound
to take care that the laws be faithfully executed. He is
Commander-in-Chief of the Army and Navy of the
United States, and of the militia of the several States
when called into the actual service of the United States.
He has no power to initiate or declare a war either
against a foreign nation or a domestic State. But by the
Act of Congress of February 28th, 1795, and 3d of
March, 1807, he is authorized to call out the militia
and use the military and naval forces of the United States
in case of invasion by foreign nations, and to suppress
insurrection against the government of a State or of the
United States.

If a war be made by invasion of a foreign nation, the
President is not only authorized but bound to resist
force by force. He does not initiate the war, but is bound
to accept the challenge without waiting for any special
legislative authority. And whether the hostile party be a
foreign invader, or States organized in rebellion, it is
none the less a war, although the declaration of it be
"unilateral." . . .

This greatest of civil wars was not gradually developed
by popular commotion, tumultuous assemblies, or local
unorganized insurrections. However long may have been
its previous conception, it nevertheless sprung forth
suddenly from the parent brain, a Minerva in the full
panoply of war. The President was bound to meet it in
the shape it presented itself, without waiting for Congress to baptize it with a name; and no name given to
it by him or them could change the fact.

It is not the less a civil war, with belligerent parties
in hostile array, because it may be called an "insurrection" by one side and the insurgents be considered as
rebels or traitors. It is not necessary that the independence of the revolted province or State be acknowledged
in order to constitute it a party belligerent in a war according to the law of nations. Foreign nations acknowledge it as war by a declaration of neutrality. The condition of neutrality cannot exist unless there be two belligerent parties. . . .

Whether the President in fulfilling his duties, as Commander-in-Chief, in suppressing an insurrection, has met

with such armed hostile resistance, and a civil war of such alarming proportions, as will compel him to accord to them the character of belligerents, is a question to be decided by him, and this Court must be governed by the decisions and acts of the political department of the Government to which this power was intrusted. "He must determine what degree of force the crisis demands." The proclamation of blockade is itself official and conclusive evidence to the Court that a state of war existed which demanded and authorized a recourse to such a measure, under the circumstances peculiar to the case.

The correspondence of Lord Lyons with the Secretary of State admits the fact and concludes the question.

If it were necessary to the technical existence of a war, that it should have a legislative sanction, we find it in almost every act passed at the extraordinary session of the legislature of 1861, which was wholly employed in enacting laws to enable the government to prosecute the war with vigor and efficiency. And finally, in 1861, we find Congress *"ex majore cautela"* and in anticipation of such astute objections, passing an act "approving, legalizing, and making valid all the acts, proclamations, and orders of the President, &c., as if they had been *issued and done under the previous express authority* and direction of the Congress of the United States."

Without admitting that such an act was necessary under the circumstances, it is plain that if the President had in any manner assumed powers which it was necessary should have the authority or sanction of Congress, that on the well known principle of law, *"omnis ratihabitio retrotrahitur et mandato equiparatur,"* this ratification has operated to perfectly cure the defect. . . .

The objection made to this act of ratification, that it is *ex post facto,* and therefore unconstitutional and void, might possibly have some weight on the trial of an indictment in a criminal Court. But precedents from that source cannot be received as authoritative in a tribunal administering the public and international law.

On this first question therefore we are of the opinion that the President had a right, *jure belli,* to institute a blockade of ports in possession of the States in rebellion, which neutrals are bound to regard. . . .

—- 10 —

EX PARTE MILLIGAN

4 Wallace 2 (1866)

It is in time of war and often in connection with the activities of the military that the great body of rights guaranteed by the Constitution are most in danger. The Constitution provides for the establishment of the machinery and procedures necessary for the waging of war, but it is in the main a peacetime document; and the courts attempt to prevent the extension of military controls into the civilian area and into the peacetime operations of government outside the strictly military field. The protections of the writ of habeas corpus, whereby courts inquire into the detention of persons claiming to be illegally held, may be suspended only in cases of rebellion or invasion. Down until the time of the Milligan case, in 1866, there had been no adequate definition of the line to be drawn between civil and military power over civilians in time of war.

Milligan, a northern civilian with southern sympathies, was arrested by the Union military forces in Indiana for what would today be called subversive activities. He was brought to trial before a military commission, with the summary procedures of such agencies and of course without a jury trial, and was sentenced to death. He sought a writ of habeas corpus on the ground that the military had no right to hold and to try him, and the case was appealed to the Supreme Court. Since military commissions for the trial of civilians in non-military areas had been provided for only by executive order and not by act of Congress, all members of the Court held the detention and the trial illegal. Four justices thought that Congress might under certain circumstances have provided for such exercise of power. The importance of the case, however, lies in the holding of the majority that such power could not be exercised at all, and in the discussion and careful delimitation of the scope of military power.

✓   ✓   ✓

[Mr. Justice Davis] . . . . The importance of the main question presented by this record cannot be overstated; for it involves the very framework of the government and the fundamental principles of American liberty.

During the late wicked Rebellion, the temper of the times did not allow that calmness in deliberation and discussion so necessary to a correct conclusion of a purely judicial question. Then, considerations of safety were mingled with the exercise of power; and feelings and interests prevailed which are happily terminated. Now that the public safety is assured, this question, as well as all others, can be discussed and decided without passion or the admixture of any element not required to form a legal judgment. We approach the investigation of this case, fully sensible of the magnitude of the inquiry and the necessity of full and cautious deliberation. . . .

The controlling question in the case is this: Upon the facts stated in Milligan's petition, and the exhibits filed, had the military commission mentioned in it jurisdiction, legally, to try and sentence him? Milligan, not a resident of one of the rebellious States, or a prisoner of war, but a citizen of Indiana for twenty years past, and never in the military or naval service, is, while at his home, arrested by the military power of the United States, imprisoned, and, on certain criminal charges preferred against him, tried, convicted, and sentenced to be hanged by a military commission, organized under the direction of the military commander of the military district of Indiana. Had this tribunal the legal power and authority to try and punish this man?

No graver question was ever considered by this court, nor one which more nearly concerns the rights of the whole people; for it is the birthright of every American citizen when charged with crime, to be tried and punished according to law. The power of punishment is alone through the means which the laws have provided for that purpose, and if they are ineffectual, there is an immunity from punishment, no matter how great an offender the individual may be, or how much his crimes may have shocked the sense of justice of the country, or endangered its safety. By the protection of the law human rights are secured; withdraw that protection, and they are at the mercy of wicked rulers, or the clamor of an excited people. If there was law to justify this military trial, it is not our province to interfere; if there was not, it is our duty to declare the nullity of the whole proceedings. The decision of this question does not depend on argument or judicial precedents, numerous and highly illustrative as they are. These precedents inform us of the extent of the struggle to preserve liberty, and to relieve those in civil life from military trials. The founders of our government were familiar with the history of that struggle, and secured in a written Constitution every right which the people had wrested from power during a contest of ages. By that Constitution and the laws authorized by it this question must be determined. The provisions of that instrument on the administration of criminal justice are too plain and direct to leave room for misconstruction or doubt of their true meaning. Those applicable to this case are found in that clause of the original Constitution which says, "That the trial of all crimes, except in case of impeachment, shall be by jury," and in the fourth, fifth, and sixth articles of the amendments. . . .

Have any of the rights guaranteed by the Constitution been violated in the case of Milligan? and if so, what are they?

Every trial involves the exercise of judicial power; and from what source did the military commission that tried him derive their authority? Certainly no part of the judicial power of the country was conferred on them; because the Constitution expressly vests it "in one supreme court and such inferior courts as the Congress may from time to time ordain and establish," and it is not pretended that the commission was a court ordained and established by Congress. They cannot justify on the mandate of the President, because he is controlled by law, and has his appropriate sphere of duty, which is to execute, not to make, the laws; and there is "no unwritten criminal code to which resort can be had as a source of jurisdiction."

But it is said that the jurisdiction is complete under the "laws and usages of war."

It can serve no useful purpose to inquire what those laws and usages are, whence they originated, where found, and on whom they operate; they can never be applied to citizens in States which have upheld the authority of the government, and where the courts are open and their process unobstructed. This court has judicial knowledge that in Indiana the Federal authority was always unopposed, and its courts always open to hear criminal accusations and redress grievances; and no usage of war could sanction a military trial there for any offense whatever of a citizen in civil life, in nowise connected with the military service. Congress could grant no such power; and to the honor of our national legislature be it said, it has never been provoked by the state of the country even to attempt its exercise. One of the plainest constitutional provisions was, therefore, infringed when Milligan was tried by a court not ordained and established by Congress, and not composed of judges appointed during good behavior. . . .

Another guarantee of freedom was broken when Milligan was denied a trial by jury. The great minds of the country have differed on the correct interpretation to be given to the various provisions of the Federal Constitution; and judicial decision has been often invoked to settle their true meaning; but until recently no one ever doubted that the right of trial by jury was fortified in the organic law against the power of attack. It is now assailed; but if ideas can be expressed in words, and language has any meaning, this right—one of the most valuable in a free country—is preserved to every one accused of crime who is not attached to the army, or navy, or militia in actual service. The sixth amendment affirms that "in all criminal prosecutions the accused shall enjoy the right to a speedy and public trial by an impartial jury,"—language broad enough to embrace all persons and cases; but the fifth, recognizing the necessity of an indictment, or presentment, before anyone can be held to answer for high crimes, "excepts cases arising in the land or naval forces, or in the militia, when in actual service, in time of war or public danger;" and the framers of the Constitution, doubtless, meant to limit the right of trial by jury, in the sixth amendment, to those persons who were subject to indictment or present-ment in the fifth. . . .

It is claimed that martial law covers with its broad mantle the proceedings of this military commission. The proposition is this: that in a time of war the commander of an armed force (if, in his opinion, the exigencies of the country demand it, and of which he is the judge) has the power, within the lines of his military district, to suspend all civil rights and their remedies, and subject citizens as well as soldiers to the rule of his will; and in the exercise of his lawful authority cannot be restrained, except by his superior officer or the President of the United States.

If this position is sound to the extent claimed, then when war exists, foreign or domestic, and the country is subdivided into military departments for mere conven-ience, the commander of one of them can, if he chooses, within his limits, on the plea of necessity, with the ap-proval of the Executive, substitute military force for, and to the exclusion of, the laws, and punish all persons, as he thinks right and proper, without fixed or certain rules.

The statement of this proposition shows its importance; for, if true, republican government is a failure, and there is an end of liberty regulated by law. Martial law, es-tablished on such a basis, destroys every guarantee of the Constitution, and effectually renders the "military in-dependent of, and superior to, the civil power,"—the attempt to do which by the King of Great Britain was deemed by our fathers such an offense, that they as-signed it to the world as one of the causes which im-pelled them to declare their independence. Civil liberty and this kind of martial law cannot endure together; the antagonism is irreconcilable and, in the conflict, one or the other must perish. . . .

It is essential to the safety of every government that

in a great crisis, like the one we have just passed through, there should be a power somewhere of suspending the writ of *habeas corpus*. In every war, there are men of previously good character, wicked enough to counsel their fellow-citizens to resist the measures deemed necessary by a good government to sustain its just authority and overthrow its enemies; and their influence may lead to dangerous combinations. In the emergency of the times, an immediate public investigation according to law may not be possible; and yet the peril to the country may be too imminent to suffer such persons to go at large. Unquestionably, there is then an exigency which demands that the government, if it should see fit, in the exercise of a proper discretion to make arrests, should not be required to produce the persons arrested in answer to a writ of *habeas corpus*. The Constitution goes no further. It does not say after a writ of *habeas corpus* is denied a citizen, that he shall be tried otherwise than by the course of the common law; if it had intended this result, it was easy by the use of direct words to have accomplished it. The illustrious men who framed that instrument were guarding the foundations of civil liberty against the abuses of unlimited power; they were full of wisdom, and the lessons of history informed them that a trial by an established court, assisted by an impartial jury, was the only sure way of protecting the citizen against oppression and wrong. Knowing this, they limited the suspension to one great right, and left the rest to remain forever inviolable. But it is insisted that the safety of the country in time of war demands that this broad claim for martial law shall be sustained. If this were true, it could be well said that a country, preserved at the sacrifice of all the cardinal principles of liberty, is not worth the cost of preservation. Happily, it is not so.

It will be borne in mind that this is not a question of the power to proclaim martial law, when war exists in a community and the courts and civil authorities are overthrown. Nor is it a question what rule a military commander, at the head of his army, can impose on States in rebellion to cripple their resources and quell the insurrection. The jurisdiction claimed is much more extensive. The necessities of the service, during the late Rebellion, required that the loyal States should be placed within the limits of certain military districts and commanders appointed in them; and, it is urged that this, in a military sense, constituted them the theatre of military operations; and, as in this case, Indiana had been and was again threatened with invasion by the enemy, the occasion was furnished to establish martial law. The conclusion does not follow from the premises. If armies were collected in Indiana, they were to be employed in another locality, where the laws were obstructed and the national authority disputed. On her soil there was no hostile foot; if once invaded, that invasion was at an end, and with it all pretext for martial law. Martial law cannot arise from a threatened invasion. The necessity must be actual and present; the invasion real, such as effectually closes the courts and deposes the civil administration. . . .

It follows, from what has been said on this subject, that there are occasions when martial rule can be properly applied. If, in foreign invasion or civil war, the courts are actually closed, and it is impossible to administer criminal justice according to law, then, on the theatre of active military operations, where war really prevails, there is a necessity to furnish a substitute for the civil authority, thus overthrown, to preserve the safety of the army and society; and as no power is left but the military, it is allowed to govern by martial rule until the laws can have their free course. As necessity creates the rule, so it limits its duration; for, if this government is continued after the courts are reinstated, it is a gross usurpation of power. Martial rule can never exist where the courts are open, and in the proper and unobstructed exercise of their jurisdiction. It is also confined to the locality of actual war. Because, during the late Rebellion it could have been enforced in Virginia, where the national authority was overturned and the courts driven out, it does not follow that it should obtain in Indiana, where that authority was never disputed, and justice was always administered. And so in the case of a foreign invasion, martial law may become a necessity in one State, when, in another, it would be "mere lawless violence." . . .

— 11 —

MISSISSIPPI v. JOHNSON

4 Wallace 475 (1867)

*The post-Civil War period brought drastic legislation
providing for military and other arbitrary forms of government in the South, the so-called Reconstruction Acts.
These measures were widely believed to be unconstitutional and attempts were made to get cases before the
Supreme Court to settle the constitutional questions.
Congress was in no mood to brook interference from the
Supreme Court, any more than from President Johnson
whom it brought to trial on impeachment charges, and
it is doubtful whether the members of the Court were
eager to invite conflict. One of the attempts made was to
get from the Supreme Court an injunction forbidding
the President to enforce the Reconstruction Acts because of their alleged unconstitutionality. For the reasons given below, the Court held that it had no power to
take such action against the President. In doing so it
provided an important discussion of the relations of the
powers of government and avoided conflict not merely
with the President but also with Congress.*

It is to be noted that in Mississippi v. Johnson *the
Supreme Court did not specifically resort to the doctrine
of political questions, which it had used in* Luther v.
Borden, *7 Howard 1 (1849) to delimit the jurisdiction
of the courts where the exercise of legislative and executive powers was involved. In the later case of* Georgia
v. Stanton, *6 Wallace 50 (1867), however, involving
issues similar to those of the Mississippi case, it did use
that doctrine to distinguish between rights of persons or
property which the courts might protect and political controversies in which the courts could not interfere, and*

thereby again avoided the constitutional question. The Court noted in that case that "the rights, for the protection of which our authority is invoked, are the rights of sovereignty, of political jurisdiction, of government, or corporate existence as a state, with all its constitutional powers and privileges. No case of private rights or private property infringed, or in danger of actual or threatened infringement, is presented by the bill . . . for the judgment of the court."

✓ ✓ ✓

[Mr. Chief Justice Chase] . . . . It is assumed by the counsel for the State of Mississippi, that the President, in the execution of the Reconstruction Acts, is required to perform a mere ministerial duty. In this assumption there is, we think, a confounding of the terms ministerial and executive, which are by no means equivalent in import.

A ministerial duty, the performance of which may, in proper cases, be required of the head of a department, by judicial process, is one in respect to which nothing is left to discretion. It is a simple, definite duty, arising under conditions admitted or proved to exist, and imposed by law. . . .

Very different is the duty of the President in the exercise of the power to see that the laws are faithfully executed, and among these laws the acts named in the bill. By the first of these acts he is required to assign generals to command in the several military districts, and to detail sufficient military force to enable such officers to discharge their duties under the law. By the supplementary acts, other duties are imposed on the several commanding generals, and these duties must necessarily be performed under the supervision of the President as commander-in-chief. The duty thus imposed on the President is in no just sense ministerial. It is purely executive and political.

An attempt on the part of the judicial department of the government to enforce the performance of such duties by the President might be justly characterized, in the language of Chief Justice Marshall, as "an absurd and excessive extravagance."

It is true that in the instance before us the interposition of the court is not sought to enforce action by the Executive under constitutional legislation, but to restrain such action under legislation alleged to be unconstitutional. But we are unable to perceive that this circumstance takes the case out of the general principles which forbid judicial interference with the exercise of Executive discretion. . . .

It will hardly be contended that Congress [the court?] can interpose, in any case, to restrain the enactment of an unconstitutional law; and yet how can the right to judicial interposition to prevent such an enactment, when the purpose is evident, and the execution of that purpose certain, be distinguished, in principle, from the right to such interposition against the execution of such a law by the President?

The Congress is the legislative department of the government; the President is the executive department. Neither can be restrained in its action by the judicial department; though the acts of both, when performed, are, in proper cases, subject to its cognizance.

The impropriety of such interference will be clearly seen upon consideration of its possible consequences.

Suppose the bill filed and the injunction prayed for allowed. If the President refuse obedience, it is needless to observe that the court is without power to enforce its process. If, on the other hand, the President complies with the order of the court and refuses to execute the acts of Congress, is it not clear that a collision may occur between the executive and legislative departments of the government? May not the House of Representatives impeach the President for such refusal? And in that case could this court interfere, in behalf of the President, thus endangered by compliance with its mandate, and restrain by injunction the Senate of the United States from sitting as a court of impeachment? Would the strange spectacle be offered to the public world of an attempt by this court to arrest proceedings in that court?

These questions answer themselves. . . .

The motion for leave to file this bill is, therefore, denied.

— 12 —

TEXAS v. WHITE

7 Wallace 700 (1869)

From the time of the adoption of the Constitution until the Civil War there was controversy over the constitutionality and the morality of attempts by states to nullify acts of the federal government or to secede from the Union. Positions varied from the argument that the Union was a voluntary aggregation of states, dissoluble at will, to the argument that the Union was indissoluble under any circumstances. The Civil War settled the controversy over secession as far as military facts were concerned. It remained for the Supreme Court to settle it as a matter of law. This it did in Texas v. White.

The case involved a dispute over the ownership of a quantity of United States bonds, which at the outbreak of the war belonged to the state of Texas. The secession government of Texas authorized the sale of certain of the bonds to finance the war against the Union. After the war, successive governors authorized suit to recover the bonds and to restrain current holders from receiving payment on them from the federal government, contending that the secession government had had no lawful power to dispose of the bonds. In order to settle the issue the Supreme Court had to decide what had been the exact status of the government of Texas during the period of the rebellion. The problems of legal strategy were difficult in view of the desire to show that, because of its rebel status, Texas had not had the power to dispose of the bonds owned by the state, and that, nevertheless, Texas, though still in the course of reconstruction, was a state in the sense that it had the right to bring a suit as a state in the Supreme Court.

By a masterly line of argument a majority of the Supreme Court managed to show that Texas had not been

*out of the Union, since by constitutional definition a
state was a unit which could not leave the Union, and
yet to show also that acts of the secession government
of Texas in aid of the rebellion had been illegal. Since
these acts had been illegal, Texas was still owner of the
bonds and, as a continuing state no longer disobedient
within the Union, it was entitled to sue in the Supreme
Court for the recovery of the bonds.*

✓   ✓   ✓

[Mr. Chief Justice Chase] . . . . The first inquiries to
which our attention was directed by counsel, arose upon
the allegations of the answer . . . (1), that no sufficient authority is shown for the prosecution of the suit
in the name and on the behalf of the State of Texas; and
(2) that the State, having severed her relations with a
majority of the States of the Union, and having by her
ordinance of secession attempted to throw off her allegiance to the Constitution and government of the
United States, has so far changed her status as to be
disabled from prosecuting suits in the National courts.

The first of these allegations is disproved by the evidence. . . .

The other allegation presents a question of jurisdiction.
It is not to be questioned that this court had original
jurisdiction of suits by States against citizens of other
States, or that the States entitled to invoke this jurisdiction must be States of the Union. But, it is equally clear
that no such jurisdiction has been conferred upon this
court of suits by any other political communities than
such States.

If, therefore, it is true that the State of Texas was not
at the time of filing this bill, or is not now, one of the
United States, we have no jurisdiction of this suit, and
it is our duty to dismiss it. . . .

It [the term "state"] describes sometimes a people or
community of individuals united more or less closely in
political relations, inhabiting temporarily or permanently
the same country; often it denotes only the country or
territorial region, inhabited by such a community; not
unfrequently it is applied to the government under which

the people live; at other times it represents the combined idea of people, territory, and government. . . .

In the Constitution the term state most frequently expresses the combined idea just noted, of people, territory, and government. A state, in the ordinary sense of the Constitution, is a political community of free citizens, occupying a territory of defined boundaries, and organized under a government sanctioned and limited by a written constitution, and established by the consent of the governed. It is the union of such states, under a common constitution, which forms the distinct and greater political unit, which that Constitution designates as the United States, and makes of the people and states which compose it one people and one country. . . .

The Republic of Texas was admitted into the Union, as a State, on the 27th of December, 1845. By this act the new State, and the people of the new State, were invested with all the rights, and became subject to all the responsibilities and duties of the original States under this Constitution.

From the date of admission, until 1861, the State was represented in the Congress of the United States by her senators and representatives, and her relations as a member of the Union remained unimpaired. In that year, acting upon the theory that the rights of a State under the Constitution might be renounced, and her obligations thrown off at pleasure, Texas undertook to sever the bond thus formed, and to break up her constitutional relations with the United States. . . .

In all respects, so far as the object could be accomplished by ordinances of the convention, by acts of the legislature, and by votes of the citizens, the relations of Texas to the Union were broken up, and new relations to a new government were established for them.

The position thus assumed could only be maintained by arms, and Texas accordingly took part, with the other Confederate States, in the war of rebellion, which these events made inevitable. During the whole of that war there was no governor, or judge, or any other State officer in Texas, who recognized the National authority. Nor was any officer of the United States permitted to exercise any authority whatever under the National government within the limits of the State except under the immediate protection of the National military forces.

Did Texas, in consequence of these acts, cease to be a State? Or, if not, did the State cease to be a member of the Union?

It is needless to discuss, at length, the question whether the right of a State to withdraw from the Union for any cause regarded by herself as sufficient is consistent with the Constitution of the United States.

The Union of the States never was a purely artificial and arbitrary relation. It began among the Colonies, and grew out of common origin, mutual sympathies, kindred principles, similar interests, and geographical relations. It was confirmed and strengthened by the necessities of war, and received definite form and character and sanction from the Articles of Confederation. By these the Union was solemnly declared to "be perpetual." And when these Articles were found to be inadequate to the exigencies of the country, the Constitution was ordained "to form a more perfect Union." It is difficult to convey the idea of indissoluble unity more clearly than by these words. What can be indissoluble if a perpetual Union, made more perfect, is not?

But the perpetuity and indissolubility of the Union by no means implies the loss of distinct and individual existence, or of the right of self-government by the States. Under the Articles of Confederation, each State retained its sovereignty, freedom, and independence, and every power, jurisdiction, and right not expressly delegated to the United States. Under the Constitution, though the powers of the States were much restricted, still, all powers not delegated to the United States, nor prohibited to the States, are reserved to the States respectively, or to the people. And we have already had occasion to remark at this term, that "the people of each State compose a State, having its own government, and endowed with all the functions essential to separate and independent existence," and that "without the States in union, there could be no such political body as the United States." County of Lane v. Oregon, 7 Wallace, 76. Not only therefore can there be no loss of separate and independent autonomy to the States, through their union under the Constitution, but it may be not unreasonably said that the preservation of the States, and the maintenance of their governments, are as much within the design and care of the Constitution as the preservation of the Union and the maintenance of the National government. The Constitution, in all its provisions, looks to an indestructible Union, composed of indestructible States.

When, therefore, Texas became one of the United States, she entered into an indissoluble relation. All the obligations of perpetual union and all the guarantees of republican government in the Union, attached at once to the State. The act which consummated her admission into the Union was something more than a compact; it was the incorporation of a new member into the political body. And it was final. The union between Texas and the other States was as complete, as perpetual, and as indissoluble as the union between the original States. There was no place for reconsideration, or revocation, except through revolution, or through consent of the States.

Considered therefore as transactions under the Constitution, the ordinance of secession, adopted by the convention and ratified by a majority of the citizens of Texas, and all the acts of her legislature intended to give effect to that ordinance, were absolutely null. They were utterly without operation in law. The obligations of the State, as a member of the Union, and of every citizen of the State, as a citizen of the United States, remained perfect and unimpaired. It certainly follows that the State did not cease to be a State, nor her citizens to be citizens of the Union. If this were otherwise, the State must have become foreign and her citizens foreigners. The war must have ceased to be a war for the suppression of rebellion, and must have become a war for conquest and subjugation.

Our conclusion therefore is, that Texas continued to be a State, and a State of the Union, notwithstanding the transactions to which we have referred. And this conclusion, in our judgment, is not in conflict with any act or declaration of any department of the National government, but entirely in accordance with the whole series

of such acts and declarations since the first outbreak of
the rebellion. . . . All admit that, during this condition
of civil war, the rights of the State as a member, and of
her people as citizens of the Union, were suspended. The
government and the citizens of the State, refusing to
recognize their constitutional obligations, assumed the
character of enemies, and incurred the consequences of
rebellion.

These new relations imposed new duties upon the
United States. The first was that of suppressing the rebellion. The next was that of reestablishing the broken relations of the State with the Union. The first of these
duties having been performed, the next necessarily engaged the attention of the National government.

The authority for the performance of the first had
been found in the power to suppress insurrection and
carry on war; for the performance of the second, authority was derived from the obligation of the United States
to guarantee to every State in the Union a republican
form of government. The latter, indeed, in the case of
a rebellion which involves the government of a State, and
for the time excludes the National authority from its
limits, seems to be a necessary complement to the
former. . . .

There being then no government in Texas in constitutional relations with the Union, it became the duty of
the United States to provide for the restoration of such
a government. . . .

Nothing in the case before us requires the court to
pronounce judgment upon the constitutionality of any
particular provision of these acts.

But it is important to observe that these acts themselves
show that the governments, which had been established
and had been in actual operation under executive direction, were recognized by Congress as provisional, as
existing, and as capable of continuance. . . .

The question of jurisdiction being thus disposed of, we
proceed to the consideration of the merits as presented
by the pleadings and the evidence. . . .

On the whole case, therefore, our conclusion is that
the State of Texas is entitled to the relief sought by her
bill, and a decee must be made accordingly.

13

LEGAL TENDER CASES

12 Wallace 457 (1871)

The Civil War created such economic strain as to threaten economic chaos. In spite of the belief, supported by experience, that a sound paper currency required adequate backing in specie, the federal government was compelled to issue paper, the so-called "greenbacks," without such backing, and to make them legal tender for the payment of debts. Although the Constitution gave power to coin money and to borrow money and to exercise other powers in the field, and to wage war and to engage in other costly activities, it made no mention of the power to issue legal tender currency. Fearing that such activity might result in runaway inflation at the hands of an irresponsible government, many hoped that the legal tender acts would be declared unconstitutional when cases finally reached the Supreme Court after the war was over. A sharply divided Court did so declare, in Hepburn v. Griswold, 8 Wallace 603 (1870). But when President Grant filled two vacancies on the Court, the two new justices joined with the former minority to hold, by a vote of five to four, that Congress had the power in question. In a part of the opinion not here quoted the Court put special emphasis on the necessities of the war situation. The shift in the Court's position brought sharp criticism of the Court's involvement in political issues.

✓   ✓   ✓

[Mr. Justice Strong] . . . . The controlling questions in these cases are the following: Are the acts of Congress, known as the Legal Tender Acts, constitutional when applied to contracts made before their passage; and, secondly, are they valid as applicable to debts contracted since their enactment? These questions have been elaborately argued, and they have received from the court that consideration which their great importance demands. It would be difficult to overestimate the consequences which must follow our decision. They will affect the entire business of the country, and take hold of the possible continued existence of the government. If it be held by this court that Congress has no constitutional power, under any circumstances, or in any emergency, to make treasury notes a legal tender for the payment of all debts (a power confessedly possessed by every independent sovereignty other than the United States), the government is without those means of self-preservation which, all must admit, may, in certain contingencies, become indispensable, even if they were not when the acts of Congress now called in question were enacted. It is also clear that if we hold the acts invalid as applicable to debts incurred, or transactions which have taken place since their enactment, our decision must cause, throughout the country, great business derangement, widespread distress, and the rankest injustice. . . . And there is no well-founded distinction to be made between the constitutional validity of an act of Congress declaring treasury notes a legal tender for the payment of debts contracted after its passage and that of an act making them a legal tender for the discharge of all debts, as well those incurred before as those made after its enactment. There may be a difference in the effects produced by the acts, and in the hardship of their operation, but in both cases the fundamental question, that which tests the validity of the legislation is, can Congress constitutionally give to treasury notes the character and qualities of money? Can such notes be constituted a legitimate circulating medium, having a defined legal value? If they can, then such notes must be available to fulfill all contracts (not expressly excepted) solvable in money, without reference to the time when the contracts were made. . . .

And here it is to be observed it is not indispensable to the existence of any power claimed for the federal government that it can be found specified in the words of the Constitution, or clearly and directly traceable to some of the specified powers. Its existence may be deduced fairly from more than one of the substantive powers expressly defined, or from them all combined. It is allowable to group together any number of them and infer from them all that the power claimed has been conferred. . . .

And it is of importance to observe that Congress has often exercised, without question, powers that are not expressly given nor ancillary to any single enumerated power. Powers thus exercised are what are called by Judge Story, in his Commentaries on the Constitution, resulting powers, arising from the aggregate powers of the government. . . .

We do not propose to dilate at length upon the circumstances in which the country was placed, when Congress attempted to make treasury notes a legal tender. They are of too recent occurrence to justify enlarged description. Suffice it to say that a civil war was then raging which seriously threatened the overthrow of the government and the destruction of the Constitution itself. It demanded the equipment and support of large armies and navies, and the employment of money to an extent beyond the capacity of all ordinary sources of supply. . . .

It was at such a time and in such an emergency that the Legal Tender Acts were passed. Now, if it were certain that nothing else would have supplied the absolute necessities of the treasury, that nothing else would have enabled the government to maintain its armies and navy, that nothing else would have saved the government and the Constitution from destruction, while the Legal Tender Acts would, could any one be bold enough to assert that Congress transgressed its powers? . . .

But if it be conceded that some other means might have been chosen for the accomplishment of these legitimate and necessary ends, the concession does not weaken the argument. It is urged now, after the lapse of nine years, and when the emergency has passed, that treasury notes without the legal tender clause might have been issued and that the necessities of the government might thus have been supplied. Hence it is inferred there was no necessity for giving to the notes issued the capability of paying private debts. At best this is mere conjecture.

But admitting it to be true, what does it prove? Nothing more than that Congress had the choice of means for a legitimate end, each appropriate, and adapted to that end, though, perhaps, in different degrees. . . .

Concluding, then, that the provision which made treasury notes a legal tender for the payment of all debts other than those expressly excepted, was not an inappropriate means for carrying into execution the legitimate powers of the government, we proceed to inquire whether it was forbidden by the letter or spirit of the Constitution. It is not claimed that any express prohibition exists, but it is insisted that the spirit of the Constitution was violated by the enactment. Here those who assert the unconstitutionality of the acts mainly rest their argument. They claim that the clause which conferred upon Congress power "to coin money, regulate the value thereof, and of foreign coins," contains an implication that nothing but that which is the subject of coinage, nothing but the precious metals can ever be declared by law to be money, or to have the uses of money. If by this is meant that because certain powers over the currency are expressly given to Congress, all other powers relating to the same subject are impliedly forbidden, we need only remark that such is not the manner in which the Constitution has always been construed. On the contrary it has been ruled that power over a particular subject may be exercised as auxiliary to an express power, though there is another express power relating to the same subject, less comprehensive. . . . To assert, then, that the clause enabling Congress to coin money and regulate its value tacitly implies a denial of all other power over the currency of the nation, is an attempt to introduce a new rule of construction against the solemn decisions of this court. So far from its containing a lurking prohibition, many have thought it was intended to confer upon Congress that general power over the currency which has always been an acknowledged attribute of sovereignty in every other civilized nation than our own, especially when considered in connection with the other clause which denies to the states the power to coin money, emit bills of credit, or make anything but gold and silver a tender in payment of debts.

14

SLAUGHTER-HOUSE CASES

16 Wallace 36 (1873)

To confirm and make permanently effective the results of the Civil War, Congress proposed for adoption the Thirteenth, Fourteenth, and Fifteenth Amendments; and in effect required the rebel states to approve those Amendments as a condition of resuming their privileges as members of the Union. The Fourteenth Amendment modified the legal doctrine of the Dred Scott case (see Document No. 8) by the provision that "All persons born or naturalized in the United States, and subject to the jurisdiction thereof, are citizens of the United States and of the State wherein they reside." In the ensuing sentence the Amendment further provided that "No State shall make or enforce any law which shall abridge the privileges or immunities of citizens of the United States; nor shall any State deprive any person of life, liberty, or property, without due process of law; nor deny to any person within its jurisdiction the equal protection of the laws."

The privileges or immunities of citizens were not defined, but to the extent of their reach the Amendment made the federal courts their guardians as against the actions of the states. Some members of the Supreme Court, steeped in belief in the balance of state power against the power of the federal government and concerned about the expansion of congressional power after the war, sought interpretations that would limit federal interference with state action. The issue arose in the Slaughter-House cases, which involved a Louisiana statute creating a monopoly of the business of slaughtering livestock in New Orleans, thereby driving other butchers out of business. Some of the latter challenged the statute on the ground that it deprived them of their privileges and immunities as citizens of the United States.

By a vote of five to four the Supreme Court virtually devitalized the privileges and immunities clause by distinguishing between the privileges which inhered in state citizenship and those inhering in national citizenship alone, and holding that the clause protected only the latter. As the opinion shows, the majority of the Court was deeply concerned about maintaining the federal balance of power. The minority, on the other hand, put emphasis on the need for protection of rights. Although the privileges and immunities clause never took on real vitality, the minority positions became the basis for later expansion of the meaning of due process and equal protection clauses.

✁   ✁   ✁

[Mr Justice Miller] . . . . The constitutional provision . . . did not create those rights, which it called privileges and immunities of citizens of the States. It threw around them in that clause no security for the citizen of the State in which they were claimed or exercised. Nor did it profess to control the power of the State governments over the rights of its own citizens.

Its sole purpose was to declare to the several States, that whatever those rights, as you grant or establish them to your own citizens, or as you limit or qualify, or impose restrictions on their exercise, the same, neither more nor less, shall be the measure of the rights of citizens of other States within your jurisdiction.

It would be the vainest show of learning to attempt to prove by citation of authority, that up to the adoption of the recent amendments, no claim or pretense was set up that those rights depended on the Federal government for their existence or protection, beyond the very few express limitations which the Federal Constitution imposed upon the States—such, for instance, as the prohibition against *ex post facto* laws, bills of attainder, and laws impairing the obligations of contracts. But with the exception of these and a few other restrictions, the entire domain of the privileges and immunities of citizens of the States, as above defined, lay within the constitutional and legislative power of the States, and without that of the Federal government. Was it the purpose of the Fourteenth Amendment, by the simple declaration that no State should make or enforce any law which shall abridge the privileges or immunities of citizens of the United States, to transfer the security and protection of all the civil rights which we have mentioned, from the States to the Federal government? And where it is declared that Congress shall have the power to enforce that article, was it intended to bring within the power of Congress the entire domain of civil rights heretofore belonging exclusively to the States?

All this and more must follow, if the proposition of the plaintiffs in error be sound. For not only are these rights subject to the control of Congress whenever in its discretion any of them are supposed to be abridged by State legislation, but that body may also pass laws in advance, limiting and restricting the exercise of legislative power by the States, in their most ordinary and usual function, as in its judgment it may think proper on all such subjects. And still further, such a construction followed by the reversal of the judgments of the Supreme Court of Louisiana in these cases, would constitute this court a perpetual censor upon all legislation of the States, on the civil rights of their own citizens, with authority to nullify such as it did not approve as consistent with those rights, as they existed at the time of the adoption of this amendment. The argument, we admit, is not always the most conclusive which is drawn from the consequences urged against the adoption of a particular construction of an instrument. But when, as in the case before us, these consequences are so serious, so far-reaching and pervading, so great a departure from the structure and spirit of our institutions; when the effect is to fetter and degrade the State governments by subjecting them to the control of Congress, in the exercise of powers heretofore universally conceded to them of the most ordinary and fundamental character; when in fact it radically changes the whole theory of the relations of the State and Federal governments to each other and of both these governments to the people; the argument has a force that is irresistible, in the absence of language which expresses such a purpose too clearly to admit of doubt.

We are convinced that no such results were intended by the Congress which proposed these amendments, nor by the legislatures of the States which ratified them. . . .

But whatever fluctuations may be seen in the history of public opinion on this subject during the period of our national existence, we think it will be found that this court, so far as its functions require, has always held with a steady and even hand the balance between State and Federal power, and we trust that such may continue to be the history of its relation to that subject so long as it shall have duties to perform which demand of it a construction of the Constitution, or any of its parts.

[Mr. Justice Field, dissenting] . . . . The Amendment was adopted to obviate objections which had been raised and pressed with great force to the validity of the civil rights act, and to place the common rights of the American citizens under the protection of the National government. . . . That Amendment was intended to give practical effect to the declaration of 1776 of inalienable rights, rights which are the gift of the Creator; which the law does not confer, but only recognizes.

[Mr. Justice Bradley, dissenting] . . . . In my view, a law which prohibits a large class of citizens from adopting a lawful employment, or from following a lawful employment previously adopted, does deprive them of liberty as well as property, without due process of law. . . . Such a law also deprives those citizens of the equal protection of the laws.

— 15 —

MUNN v. ILLINOIS

94 U.S. 113 (1877)

With the expansion of railroads and other forms of enterprise, states began increasingly to regulate in the public interest. Business interests, in turn, sought to es-

cape or curtail state regulation by reliance on their rights under the due process and equal protection clauses of the Fourteenth Amendment. The Supreme Court at first looked askance at such attempts to escape regulation, and in terms of the doctrine of "business affected with a public interest" it justified the exercise of state power. Although the Court gradually shifted its ground to increased restriction of state power, its initial statement of the power to regulate is historically important.

The Munn case involved an Illinois statute fixing the maximum rates which privately owned grain elevators in Chicago might charge for the storage of grain. Since the owners of grain shipped from many states had to make use of the Chicago facilities, the owners of the elevators were in position to exact exorbitant rates for storage. The operators, on the other hand, contended that since their property was strictly private the regulation of rates violated the Fourteenth Amendment. The Supreme Court, however, found this business so related to the public interest that regulation was not unconstitutional.

✓   ✓   ✓

[Mr. Chief Justice Waite] . . . . When one becomes a member of society, he necessarily parts with some rights or privileges which, as an individual not affected by his relations to others, he might retain. "A body politic," as aptly defined in the preamble of the Constitution of Massachusetts, "is a social compact by which the whole people covenants with each citizen, and each citizen with the whole people, that all shall be governed by certain laws for the common good." This does not confer power upon the whole people to control rights which are purely and exclusively private . . . but it does authorize the establishment of laws requiring each citizen to so conduct himself and so use his own property, as not unnecessarily to injure another. . . .

From this it is apparent that, down to the time of the adoption of the Fourteenth Amendment, it was not supposed that statutes regulating the use, or even the price of the use, of private property necessarily deprived an owner of his property without due process of law. Under some circumstances they may, but not under all. The

amendment does not change the law in this particular:
it simply prevents the States from doing that which will
operate as such a deprivation.

This brings us to inquire as to the principles upon
which this power of regulation rests, in order that we
may determine what is within and what is without its
operative effect. Looking, then, to the common law,
from whence came the right which the Constitution pro-
tects, we find that when private property is "affected
with a public interest, it ceases to be *juris privati* only."
This was said by Lord Chief Justice Hale more than
two hundred years ago, in his treatise *De Portibus Maris*
. . . and has been accepted without objection as an
essential element in the law of property ever since. Property does become clothed with a public interest when
used in a manner to make it of public consequence, and
affect the community at large. When, therefore, one de-
votes his property to a use in which the public has an
interest, he, in effect, grants to the public an interest in
that use, and must submit to be controlled by the public for the common good, to the extent of the interest he
has thus created. He may withdraw his grant by discon-
tinuing the use; but, so long as he maintains the use,
he must submit to the control. . . .

From the same source comes the power to regulate the
charges of common carriers, which was done in England
as long ago as the third year of the reign of William and
Mary, and continued until within a comparatively recent
period. . . .

But we need not go further. Enough has already been
said to show that, when private property is devoted to a
public use, it is subject to public regulation. It remains
only to ascertain whether the warehouses of these plaintiffs in error, and the business which is carried on there,
come within the operation of this principle. . . .

Under such circumstances it is difficult to see why, if
the common carrier, or the miller, or the ferryman, or
the innkeeper, or the wharfinger, or the baker, or the
cartman, or the hackney-coachman, pursues a public
employment and exercises "a sort of public office," these
plaintiffs in error do not. They stand, to use again the
language of their counsel, in the very "gateway of commerce," and take toll from all who pass. Their business

most certainly "tends to a common charge, and is become a thing of public interest and use." Every bushel of grain for its passage "pays a toll, which is a common charge," and, therefore, according to Lord Hale, every such warehouseman "ought to be under public regulation, viz., that he . . . take but reasonable toll." Certainly, if any business can be clothed "with a public interest and cease to be *juris privati* only," this has been. It may not be made so by the operation of the Constitution of Illinois or this statute, but it is by the facts. . . . To limit the rate of charge for services rendered in a public employment, or for the use of property in which the public has an interest, is only changing a regulation which existed before. It establishes no new principle in the law, but only gives a new effect to an old one.

We know that this is a power which may be abused; but that is no argument against its existence. For protection against abuses by Legislatures the people must resort to the polls, not to the courts.

— 16 —

CIVIL RIGHTS CASES

109 U.S. 3 (1883)

In the attempt to secure to Negroes the full rights of citizenship the Fourteenth Amendment incorporated the several provisions quoted above (see Document No. 14), *and provided also that "The Congress shall have power to enforce, by appropriate legislation, the provisions of this article." On the basis of these and other provisions Congress enacted broad protections of civil rights. The Civil Rights Act of 1875 gave equal rights to use of inns, theaters, public conveyances, and other facilities. By the time when cases involving the act reached the*

*Supreme Court, in 1883, much of the country had grown
weary of the perennial difficulties of giving protection
to Negroes against discrimination. In this atmosphere of
disillusionment, the Supreme Court held that the Fourteenth Amendment had not given Congress substantive
power to protect civil rights but only power to correct
abuses by the states. By this decision Congress was relieved of its basic obligation for the protection of the civil
rights of Negroes. Again the Court showed itself more
concerned with the federal balance of power than with
substantive rights.*

[Mr. Justice Bradley] . . . . It is State action of a
particular character that is prohibited. Individual invasion of individual rights is not the subject-matter of the
amendment. It has a deeper and broader scope. It nulli-
fies and makes void all State legislation, and State action
of every kind, which impairs the privileges and immunities of citizens of the United States, or which injures
them in life, liberty or property without due process of
law, or which denies to any of them the equal protection
of the laws. It not only does this, but, in order that the
national will, thus declared, may not be a mere *brutum
fulmen,* the last section of the amendment invests Congress with power to enforce it by appropriate legislation.
To enforce what? To enforce the prohibition. To adopt
appropriate legislation for correcting the effects of such
prohibited State laws and State acts, and thus to render
them effectually null, void, and innocuous. This is the
legislative power conferred upon Congress, and this is
the whole of it. It does not invest Congress with power
to legislate upon subjects which are within the domain
of State legislation; but to provide modes of relief
against State legislation, or State action, of the kind referred to. It does not authorize Congress to create a
code of municipal law for the regulation of private
rights; but to provide modes of redress against the operation of State laws, and the action of State officers executive or judicial, when these are subversive of the fundamental rights specified in the amendment. Positive
rights and privileges are undoubtedly secured by the

Fourteenth Amendment; but they are secured by way of prohibition against State laws and State proceedings affecting those rights and privileges, and by power given to Congress to legislate for the purpose of carrying such prohibition into effect; and such legislation must necessarily be predicated upon such supposed State laws or State proceedings, and be directed to the correction of their operation and effect. . . .

If this legislation is appropriate for enforcing the prohibitions of the amendment, it is difficult to see where it is to stop. Why may not Congress with equal show of authority enact a code of laws for the enforcement and vindication of all rights of life, liberty, and property? If it is supposable that the States may deprive persons of life, liberty, and property without due process of law and the amendment itself does not suppose this, why should not Congress proceed at once to prescribe due process of law for the protection of every one of these fundamental rights, in every possible case, as well as to prescribe equal privileges in inns, public conveyances, and theatres? . . . The assumption is certainly unsound. It is repugnant to the Tenth Amendment of the Constitution, which declares that powers not delegated to the United States by the Constitution, nor prohibited by it to the States, are reserved to the States respectively or to the people. . . .

In this connection it is proper to state that civil rights, such as are guaranteed by the Constitution against State aggression, cannot be impaired by the wrongful acts of individuals, unsupported by State authority in the shape of laws, customs, or judicial or executive proceedings. The wrongful act of an individual, unsupported by any such authority, is simply a private wrong, or a crime of that individual; an invasion of the rights of the injured party, it is true, whether they affect his person, his property, or his reputation; but if not sanctioned in some way by the State, or not done under State authority, his rights remain in full force, and may presumably be vindicated by resort to the laws of the State for redress. . . .

We must not forget that the province and scope of the Thirteenth and Fourteenth Amendments are different; the former simply abolished slavery: the latter prohibited the States from abridging the privileges or immunities of citizens of the United States, from depriving them of life, liberty, or property without due process of law, and from denying to any the equal protection of the laws. The amendments are different, and the powers of Congress under them are different. What Congress has power to do under one, it may not have power to do under the other. Under the Thirteenth Amendment, it has only to do with slavery and its incidents. Under the Fourteenth Amendment, it has power to counteract and render nugatory all State laws and proceedings which have the effect to abridge any of the privileges and immunities of citizens of the United States, or to deprive them of life, liberty, or property without due process of law, or to deny to any of them the equal protection of the laws. Under the Thirteenth Amendment, the legislation, so far as necessary or proper to eradicate all forms and incidents of slavery and involuntary servitude, may be direct and primary, operating upon the acts of individuals, whether sanctioned by State legislation or not; under the Fourteenth, as we have already shown, it must necessarily be, and can only be, corrective in its character, addressed to counteract and afford relief against State regulations or proceedings. . . .

When a man has emerged from slavery, and by the aid of beneficent legislation has shaken off the inseparable concomitants of that state, there must be some stage in the progress of his elevation when he takes the rank of a mere citizen, and ceases to be the special favorite of the laws, and when his rights, as a citizen or a man, are to be protected in the ordinary modes by which other men's rights are protected. . . .

[Mr. Justice Harlan, dissenting] . . . . I cannot resist the conclusion that the substance and spirit of the recent Amendment of the Constitution have been sacrificed by a subtle and ingenious verbal criticism.

POLLOCK v. FARMERS' LOAN & TRUST COMPANY

158 U.S. 601 (1895)

The period of the late 1880's and early 1890's witnessed a great deal of popular discontent with the inequality of income and opportunity and a great deal of effort to equalize conditions through currency control, tariff adjustment, and changes in tax laws. Under the pressure of this discontent, Congress in 1894 enacted a federal income tax law with exemption of lower incomes so that well-to-do people were called on to pay an increased proportion of the cost of the federal government. Wealthy and conservative people, frightened already by the Populist Movement, regarded the new tax as the first step in a dangerous drift toward socialism. Although a federal income tax had been in force during the Civil War and for a time thereafter, and had been found constitutional by the Supreme Court, a concerted effort was now made to persuade the Court that such a measure was unconstitutional.

The strategy was to persuade the Court that an income tax was a direct tax, rather than an indirect or excise tax as it had hitherto been classified. If it was a direct tax, it could be collected constitutionally only by apportioning the amount to be collected among the several states according to population. Since the larger incomes were earned in a few states, apportionment would largely defeat the purpose of requiring wealth to pay its way. The Court, in part sympathetic with the conservative view, decided that a tax on rents was the same as a tax on the property from which the rents were collected, and was therefore a direct tax. One justice being absent, certain other questions were presented at a reargument, when

*the Court, voting five to four, held that a tax on income
from personal property was also a direct tax. Hence, a
tax on income from property of any kind could be collected only by apportionment among the several states
according to population, and the present statute was
unconstitutional. The decision brought so much protest
that it resulted eventually in adoption of the Sixteenth
Amendment authorizing collection of income taxes without apportionment.*

✓   ✓   ✓

[Mr. Chief Justice Fuller] . . . . Whatever the speculative views of political economists or revenue reform-
ers may be, can it be properly held that the Constitution, taken in its plain and obvious sense, and with due
regard to the circumstances attending the formation of
the government, authorizes a general unapportioned tax
on the products of the farm and the rents of real estate,
although imposed merely because of ownership and with
no possible means of escape from payment, as belonging to a totally different class from that which includes
the property from whence the income proceeds?

There can be but one answer, unless the constitutional
restriction is to be treated as utterly illusory and futile,
and the object of its framers defeated. We find it impossible to hold that a fundamental requisition, deemed
so important as to be enforced by two provisions, one
affirmative and one negative, can be refined away by
forced distinctions between that which gives value to
property, and the property itself.

Nor can we perceive any ground why the same reasoning does not apply to capital in personalty held for
the purpose of income or ordinarily yielding income,
and to the income therefrom. All the real estate of the
country, and all its invested personal property, are open
to the direct operation of the taxing power if an apportionment be made according to the Constitution. The
Constitution does not say that no direct tax shall be
laid by apportionment on any other property than land;
on the contrary, it forbids all unapportioned direct taxes;
and we know of no warrant for excepting personal property from the exercise of the power, or any reason why
an apportioned direct tax cannot be laid and assessed,

as Mr. Gallatin said in his report when Secretary of the Treasury in 1812, "upon the same objects of taxation on which the direct taxes levied under the authority of the State are laid and assessed." . . .

We have unanimously held in this case that, so far as this law operates on the receipts from municipal bonds, it cannot be sustained, because it is a tax on the power of the States, and on their instrumentalities to borrow money, and consequently repugnant to the Constitution. But if, as contended, the interest when received has become merely money in the recipient's pocket, and taxable as such without reference to the source from which it came, the question is immaterial whether it should have been originally taxed at all or not. This was admitted by the Attorney General with characteristic candor; and it follows that, if the revenue derived from municipal bonds cannot be taxed because the source cannot be, the same rule applies to revenue from any other source not subject to the tax; and the lack of power to levy any but an apportioned tax on real estate and personal property equally exists as to the revenue therefrom.

Admitting that this act taxes the income of property irrespective of its source, still we cannot doubt that such a tax is necessarily a direct tax in the meaning of the Constitution. . . .

Being direct, and therefore to be laid by apportionment, is there any real difficulty in doing so? Cannot Congress, if the necessity exists of raising thirty, forty, or any other number of million dollars for the support of the government, in addition to the revenue from duties, imposts, and excises, apportion the quota of each State upon the basis of the census, and thus advise it of the payment which must be made, and proceed to assess that amount on all the real or personal property and the income of all persons in the State, and collect the same if the State does not in the meantime assume and pay its quota and collect the amount according to its own system and in its own way? Cannot Congress do this, as respects either or all these subjects of taxation, and deal with each in such manner as might be deemed expedient, as indeed was done in the act of July 14, 1798, c.75, 1 Stat. 597? Inconveniences might possibly attend the levy of an income tax, notwithstanding the listing of receipts, when adjusted, furnishes its own valuation; but that it is apportionable is hardy denied, although it is asserted that it would operate so unequally as to be undesirable. . . .

We have considered the act only in respect to the tax on income derived from real estate, and from invested personal property, and have not commented on so much of it as bears on gains or profits from business, privileges, or employments, in view of the instances in which taxation on business, privileges, or employments has assumed the guise of an excise tax and been sustained as such. . . .

Our conclusions may, therefore, be summed up as follows:

First. We adhere to the opinion already announced, that, taxes on real estate being indisputably direct taxes, taxes on the rents or incomes of real estate are equally direct taxes.

Second. We are of opinion that taxes on personal property, or on the income of personal property, are likewise direct taxes. . . .

— 18 —

PLESSY v. FERGUSON

163 U.S. 537 (1896)

A third of a century after the Civil War, discrimination of various kinds still continued against Negroes in the former slave states, and their constitutional rights in various areas remained undetermined. One such discriminatory measure was an act of the legislature of Louisiana, which required all railroads to provide "equal but separate" accommodations for members of the white and black races and forbade intermingling. A Negro challenge to the constitutionality of the statute led to the famous "separate but equal" decision, to which only Justice Harlan dissented. The decision remained the law of the land until overruled in Brown v. Board of Education (see Document No. 32).

✓   ✓   ✓

[Mr. Justice Brown] . . . . The constitutionality of this act is attacked upon the ground that it conflicts both with the Thirteenth Amendment of the Constitution, abolishing slavery, and the Fourteenth Amendment, which prohibits certain restrictive legislation on the part of the States.

1. That it does not conflict with the Thirteenth Amendment, which abolished slavery and involuntary servitude, except as a punishment for crime, is too clear for argument. . . .

2. By the Fourteenth Amendment, all persons born or naturalized in the United States, and subject to the jurisdiction thereof, are made citizens of the United States and of the State wherein they reside; and the States are forbidden from making or enforcing any law which shall abridge the privileges or immunities of citizens of the United States, or shall deprive any person of life, liberty or property without due process of law, or deny to any person within their jurisdiction the equal protection of the laws. . . .

The object of the amendment was undoubtedly to enforce the absolute equality of the two races before the law, but in the nature of things it could not have been intended to abolish distinctions based upon color, or to enforce social, as distinguished from political equality, or a commingling of the two races upon terms unsatisfactory to either. Laws permitting, and even requiring, their separation in places where they are liable to be brought into contact do not necessary imply the inferiority of either race to the other, and have been generally, if not universally, recognized as within the competency of the state legislatures in the exercise of their police power. The most common instance of this is connected with the establishment of separate schools for white and colored children, which has been held to be a valid exercise of the legislative power even by courts of States where the political rights of the colored race have been longest and most earnestly enforced.

One of the earliest of these cases is that of Robert v. City of Boston, 5 Cush. 198, in which the Supreme Judicial Court of Massachusetts held that the general school committee of Boston had power to make provisions for the instruction of colored children in separate schools established exclusively for them, and to prohibit their attendance upon the other schools. . . .

The distinction between laws interfering with the political equality of the negro and those requiring the separation of the two races in schools, theatres, and railway carriages has been frequently drawn by this court. . . .

So far, then, as a conflict with the Fourteenth Amendment is concerned, the case reduces itself to the question whether the statute of Louisiana is a reasonable regulation, and with respect to this there must necessarily be a large discretion on the part of the legislature. In determining the question of reasonableness it is at liberty to act with reference to the established usages, customs and traditions of the people, and with a view to the promotion of their comfort, and the preservation of the public peace and good order. Gauged by this standard, we cannot say that a law which authorizes or even requires the separation of the two races in public conveyances is unreasonable, or more obnoxious to the Fourteenth Amendment than the acts of Congress requiring separate schools for colored children in the District of Columbia, the constitutionality of which does not seem to have been questioned, or the corresponding acts of state legislatures.

We consider the underlying fallacy of the plaintiff's argument to consist in the assumption that the enforced separation of the two races stamps the colored race with a badge of inferiority. If this be so, it is not by reason of anything found in the act, but solely because the colored race chooses to put that construction upon it. . . . The argument also assumed that social prejudices may be overcome by legislation, and that equal rights cannot be secured to the negro except by an enforced commingling of the two races. We cannot accept this proposition. If the two races are to meet upon terms of

social equality, it must be the result of natural affinities,
a mutual appreciation of each other's merits and a voluntary consent of individuals. As was said by the Court of
Appeals of New York in People v. Gallagher, 93 N.Y.
438, 448, "this end can neither be accomplished nor
promoted by laws which conflict with the general sentiment of the community upon whom they are designed
to operate." . . . Legislation is powerless to eradicate
racial instincts or to abolish distinctions based upon
physical differences, and the attempt to do so can only
result in accentuating the difficulties of the present situation. If the civil and political rights of both races be
equal one cannot be inferior to the other civilly or po-
litically. If one race be inferior to the other socially,
the Constitution of the United States cannot put them
upon the same plane.

[Mr. Justice Harlan, dissenting] . . . . Our Constitution is color-blind, and neither knows nor tolerates
classes among citizens. In respect of civil rights, all citizens are equal before the law. . . .

In my opinion, the judgment this day rendered will,
in time, prove to be quite as pernicious as the decision
made by this tribunal in the Dred Scott Case.

— 19 —

SMYTH v. AMES

169 U.S. 466 (1898)

For a number of years after the decision in Munn *v.*
Illinois *(see Document No. 15) the Supreme Court
drifted steadily away from its position that people at the
polls, and not courts, were to provide protection against
the abuses of legislative regulation. Although as to businesses affected with a public interest legislatures could*

*fix charges, it became the rule that the courts became
the arbiters of the reasonableness of rates fixed and that
in order to be constitutional the rate level must permit
the earning of a fair return on the fair value of the property involved. The percentage of profit regarded by the
Supreme Court as a fair return varied from time to time
and situation to situation. The criteria for the measure
of the value of property were also variables. In the so-
called rule of* Smyth v. Ames *the Court displayed the
utter indefiniteness of the variables and provided a basis
for shifting criteria which for a third of a century kept
the public utilities of the country in a welter of litigation
over constantly changing rate structures. Only gradually
in recent years has the Court given up the requirement
of fair return on a fair value with all its uncertainties.*

✓   ✓   ✓

[Mr. Justice Harlan] . . . . By the Fourteenth Amendment it is provided that no State shall deprive any person of property without due process of law, nor deny
to any person within its jurisdiction the equal protection
of the laws. . . . What amounts to deprivation of property without due process of law or what is a denial of
the equal protection of the laws is often difficult to determine, especially where the question relates to the
property of a *quasi* public corporation and the extent to
which it may be subjected to public control. . . .

In view of the adjudications these principles must be
regarded as settled.

1. A railroad corporation is a person within the meaning of the Fourteenth Amendment declaring that no
State shall deprive any person of property without due
process of law, nor deny to any person within its jurisdiction the equal protection of the laws.

2. A state enactment, or regulation made under the
authority of a state enactment, establishing rates for the
transportation of persons or property by railroad that
will not admit of the carrier earning such compensation
as under all the circumstances is just to it and to the
public, would deprive such carrier of its property without due process of law and deny to it the equal protection of the laws, and would therefore be repugnant to

the Fourteenth Amendment to the Constitution of the United States.

3. While rates for the transportation of persons and property within the limits of a State are primarily for its determination, the question whether they are so unreasonably low as to deprive the carrier of its property without such compensation as the Constitution secures, and therefore without due process of law, cannot be so conclusively determined by the legislature of the State or by regulations adopted under its authority, that the matter may not become the subject of judicial inquiry. . . .

The reasonableness or unreasonableness of rates prescribed by a State for the transportation of persons and property wholly within its limits must be determined without reference to the interstate business done by the carrier, or to the profits derived from it. The State cannot justify unreasonably low rates for domestic transportation, considered alone, upon the ground that the carrier is earning large profits on its interstate business, over which, so far as rates are concerned, the State has no control. . . .

The plaintiffs contended that a railroad company is entitled to exact such charges for transportation as will enable it, at all times, not only to pay operating expenses, but also to meet the interest regularly accruing upon all its outstanding obligations, and justify a dividend upon all its stock; and that to prohibit it from maintaining rates or charges for transportation adequate to all those ends will deprive it of its property without due process of law, and deny to it the equal protection of the laws. . . .

The broad proposition advanced by counsel involves some misconception of the relations between the public and a railroad corporation. It is unsound in that it practically excludes from consideration the fair value of the property used, omits altogether any consideration of the right of the public to be exempt from unreasonable exactions, and makes the interests of the corporation maintaining a public highway the sole test in determining whether the rates established by or for it are such as may be rightfully prescribed as between it and the public. A railroad is a public highway, and none the less so because constructed and maintained through the agency of a corporation deriving its existence and powers from the State. Such a corporation was created for public purposes. It performs a function of the State. Its authority to exercise the right of eminent domain and to charge tolls was given primarily for the benefit of the public. It is under governmental control though such control must be exercised with due regard to the constitutional guarantees for the protection of its property. . . .

If a railroad corporation has bonded its property for an amount that exceeds its fair value, or if its capitalization is largely fictitious, it may not impose upon the public the burden of such increased rates, as may be required for the purpose of realizing profits upon such excessive valuation or fictitious capitalization; and the apparent value of the property and franchises used by the corporation, as represented by its stocks, bonds and obligations, is not alone to be considered when determining the rates that may be reasonably charged. . . .

The basis of all calculations as to the reasonableness of rates to be charged by a corporation maintaining a highway under legislative sanction must be the fair value of the property being used by it for the convenience of the public. And in order to ascertain that value the original cost of construction, the amount expended in permanent improvements, the amount and market value of its bonds and stock, the present as compared with the original cost of construction, the probable earning capacity of the property under particular rates prescribed by statute, and the sum required to meet operating expenses, are all matters for consideration, and are to be given such weight as may be just and right in each case. We do not say that there may not be other matters to be regarded in estimating the value of the property. What the company is entitled to ask is a fair return upon the value of that which it employs for the public convenience. On the other hand, what the public is entitled to demand is that no more be exacted from it for the use of a public highway than the services rendered by it are reasonably worth. . . .

— 20 —

LOCHNER v. NEW YORK

198 U.S. 45 (1905)

Although the courts recognized the power of the states to enact measures limiting freedom of activity and the rights of property when such limitation was necessary to the health, morals, safety, and welfare of the people, the due process clause of the Fourteenth Amendment was used to insure a broad area of freedom. The clause, in other words, became an instrument of laissez faire. An important example was the Supreme Court's decision in Lochner v. New York *and the much-quoted dissenting opinion of Justice Holmes. As a health measure, a New York statute forbade employment of any person in a bakery or confectionery shop for more than sixty hours a week. The Supreme Court, stating that the right of a person to make contracts in relation to his business was part of the liberty of the individual protected by the Fourteenth Amendment, found the statute unconstitutional as a violation of the freedom of contract. During the years ahead the Court gave way as to regulation of the hours of labor, but for a long period it held tenaciously to the immunity of wages until eventually compelled to give way even there.*

✦   ✦   ✦

[Mr. Justice Peckham] . . . . Contracts in violation of a statute, either of the Federal or State government, or a contract to let one's property for immoral purposes, or to do any other unlawful act, could obtain no protection from the Federal Constitution, as coming under the liberty of person or of free contract. Therefore, when the State, by its legislature, in the assumed exercise of its police powers, has passed an act which seriously limits the right to labor or the right of contract in regard

105

to their means of livelihood between persons who are *sui juris* (both employer and employee), it becomes of great importance to determine which shall prevail—the right of the individual to labor for such time as he may choose, or the right of the State to prevent the individual from laboring or from entering into contracts to labor, beyond a certain time prescribed by the State.

This court has recognized the existence and upheld the exercise of the police powers of the States in many cases which might fairly be considered as border ones, and it has, in the course of its determination of questions regarding the asserted invalidity of such statutes, on the ground of their violation of the rights secured by the Federal Constitution, been guided by rules of a very liberal nature, the application of which has resulted, in numerous instances, in upholding the validity of state statutes thus assailed. . . .

It must, of course, be conceded that there is a limit to the valid exercise of the police power by the State. . . . In every case that comes before this court, therefore, where legislation of this character is concerned and where the protection of the Federal Constitution is sought, the question necessarily arises: Is this a fair, reasonable and appropriate exercise of the police power of the State, or is it an unreasonable, unnecessary and arbitrary interference with the right of the individual to his personal liberty or to enter into those contracts in relation to labor which may seem to him appropriate or necessary for the support of himself and his family? Of course the liberty of contract relating to labor includes both parties to it. The one has as much right to purchase as the other to sell labor.

This is not a question of substituting the judgment of the court for that of the legislature. If the act be within the power of the State it is valid, although the judgment of the court might be totally opposed to the enactment of such a law. But the question would still remain: Is it within the police power of the State? and that question must be answered by the court.

The question whether this act is valid as a labor law, pure and simple, may be dismissed in a few words. There is no reasonable ground for interfering with the lib-

erty of person or the right of free contract, by determining the hours of labor, in the occupation of a baker.
There is no contention that bakers as a class are not
equal in intelligence and capacity to men on other trades
or manual occupations, or that they are not able to assert
their rights and care for themselves without the protecting arm of the State, interfering with their independence
of judgment and of action. They are in no sense wards
of the State. . . .

The law must be upheld, if at all, as a law pertaining
to the health of the individual engaged in the occupation
of a baker. It does not affect any other portion of the
public than those who are engaged in that occupation.
Clean and wholesome bread does not depend upon
whether the baker works but ten hours per day or only
sixty hours a week. The limitation of the hours of labor does not come within the police power on that
ground. . . .

We think that there can be no fair doubt that the trade
of a baker, in and of itself, is not an unhealthy one to
that degree which would authorize the legislature to
interfere with the right to labor, and with the right of
free contract on the part of the individual, either as
employer or employee. In looking through statistics regarding all trade and occupations, it may be true that
the trade of a baker does not appear to be as healthy as
some other trades, and is also vastly more healthy than
still others. To the common understanding the trade of
a baker has never been regarded as an unhealthy one.
Very likely physicians would not recommend the exercise of that or of any other trade as a remedy for ill
health. Some occupations are more healthy than others,
but we think there are none which might not come under the power of the legislature to supervise and control
the hours of working therein, if the mere fact that the
occupation is not absolutely and perfectly healthy is to
confer that right upon the legislative department of the
government. It might be safely affirmed that almost all
occupations more or less affect the health. . . . But are
we all, on that account, at the mercy of the legislative
majorities?

Statutes of the nature of that under review, limiting

the hours in which grown and intelligent men may labor to earn their living, are mere meddlesome interferences with the rights of the individual, and they are not saved from condemnation by the claim that they are passed in the exercise of the police power and upon the subject of the health of the individual whose rights are interfered with, unless there be some fair ground, reasonable in and of itself, to say that there is material danger to the public health or to the health of the employees, if the hours of labor are not curtailed. If this be not clearly the case the individuals, whose rights are thus made the subject of legislative interference, are under the protection of the Federal Constitution regarding their liberty of contract as well as of person; and the legislature of the State has no power to limit their rights as proposed in this statute. . . .

It was further urged on the argument that restricting the hours of labor in the case of bakers was valid because it tended to cleanliness on the part of the workers, as a man was more apt to be cleanly when not overworked, and if cleanly then his "output" was also more likely to be so. . . . In our judgment it is not possible in fact to discover the connection between the number of hours a baker may work in the bakery and the healthy quality of the bread made by the workman. The connection, if any exists, is too shadowy and thin to build any argument for the interference of the legislature. If the man works ten hours a day it is all right, but if ten and a half or eleven his health is in danger and his bread unhealthful, and, therefore, he shall not be permitted to do it. This, we think, is unreasonable and entirely arbitrary. . . .

It is impossible for us to shut our eyes to the fact that many of the laws of this character, while passed under what is claimed to be the police power for the purpose of protecting the public health or welfare, are, in reality, passed from other motives. We are justified in saying so when, from the character of the law, and the subject upon which it legislates, it is apparent that the public health or welfare bears but the most remote relation to the law. The purpose of a statute must be determined from the natural and legal effect of the language employed; and whether it is or is not repugnant to the Constitution of the United States must be determined from the natural effect of such statutes when put into operation, and not from their proclaimed purpose. . . .

[Mr. Justice Holmes, dissenting] . . . . This case is decided upon an economic theory which a large part of the country does not entertain. If it were a question whether I agreed with that theory, I should desire to study it further and long before making up my mind. But I do not conceive that to be my duty, because I strongly believe that my agreement or disagreement has nothing to do with the right of a majority to embody their opinions in law. . . . The Fourteenth Amendment does not enact Mr. Herbert Spencer's Social Statics. . . . A constitution is not intended to embody a particular economic theory, whether of paternalism and the organic relation of the citizen to the state or of *laissez faire*. It is made for people of fundamentally differing views, and the accident of our finding certain opinions natural and familiar, or novel, and even shocking, ought not to conclude our judgment upon the question whether statutes embodying them conflict with the Constitution of the United States.

General propositions do not decide concrete cases. The decision will depend on a judgment or intuition more subtle than any articulate major premise. But I think that the proposition just stated, if it is accepted, will carry us toward the end. Every opinion tends to become a law. I think that the word liberty in the Fourteenth Amendment is perverted when it is held to prevent the natural outcome of a dominant opinion, unless it can be said that a rational and fair man necessarily would admit that the statute proposed would infringe fundamental principles as they have been understood by the traditions of our people and our law. . . .

— 21 —

HAMMER v. DAGENHART

247 U.S. 251 (1918)

The rapid and steady growth in the dimensions of commerce across state lines meant that by the early years of the twentieth century the federal government, in the process of regulating interstate commerce, was inevitably dealing with matters which hitherto would have been left primarily to regulation by the states or left free of regulation. Since evils involved in interstate shipments could be reached only in part by any one state, no state having jurisdiction beyond its own lines, it was only natural that people should look to the federal government for the solution of interstate problems. Congress provided, and the Supreme Court upheld, federal regulation of the interstate aspects of lotteries, food and drug shipments that might involve impurities or deception of customers, narcotic traffic, white slave traffic, and other matters. But when Congress forbade shipment in interstate commerce of goods produced by child labor, about the morality of which there were differing opinions, the Court resorted to laissez faire theories and theories of state rights to strike down the statute, by the narrow margin of five to four. The excerpt from the dissenting opinion indicates the nature of minority feeling.

It should be noted that Congress tried again to restrict child labor by exercise of the taxing power and was again defeated by the Supreme Court. Thereafter Congress proposed to the states a constitutional amendment giving the power to prohibit child labor. The amendment was ratified in a number of states but never by the requisite three-fourths of them. Finally, with the change in public sentiment which came with the New Deal period, the Supreme Court in United States v. Darby, *312 U.S. 100 (1941) overruled the case here presented, so that Congress could regulate child labor connected with interstate commerce without the necessity for a constitutional amendment.*

✓ ✓ ✓

[Mr. Justice Day] . . . . The attack upon the act rests upon three propositions: First: It is not a regulation of interstate and foreign commerce; Second: It contravenes the Tenth Amendment to the Constitution; Third: It conflicts with the Fifth Amendment to the Constitution.

The controlling question for decision is: Is it within the authority of Congress in regulating commerce among the States to prohibit the transportation in interstate commerce of manufactured goods, the product of a factory in which, within thirty days prior to their removal therefrom, children under the age of fourteen have been employed or permitted to work, or children between the ages of fourteen and sixteen years have been employed or permitted to work more than eight hours in any day, or more than six days in any week, or after the hour of 7 o'clock P.M. or before the hour of 6 o'clock A.M.?

The power essential to the passage of this act, the Government contends, is found in the commerce clause of the Constitution which authorizes Congress to regulate commerce with foreign nations and among the States.

In Gibbons v. Ogden, 9 Wheat. 1, Chief Justice Marshall, speaking for this court, and defining the extent and nature of the commerce power, said, "It is the power to regulate, that is, to prescribe the rule by which commerce is to be governed." In other words, the power is one to control the means by which commerce is carried on, which is directly the contrary of the assumed right to forbid commerce from moving and thus destroy it as to particular commodities. But it is insisted that adjudged cases in this court establish the doctrine that the power to regulate given to Congress incidentally includes the authority to prohibit the movement of ordinary commodities and therefore that the subject is not open for discussion. The cases demonstrate the contrary. They rest upon the character of the particular subjects dealt with and the fact that the scope of governmental authority, state or national, possessed over them is such that the authority to prohibit is as to them but the exertion of the power to regulate. . . . The thing intended to be accomplished by this statute is the denial of the facilities of interstate commerce to those manufacturers in the States who employ children within the prohibited ages. The act in its effect does not regulate transportation among the States, but aims to standardize the ages at which children may be employed in mining and manufacturing within the States. The goods shipped are of themselves harmless. The act permits them to be freely shipped after thirty days from the time of their removal from the factory. When offered for shipment, and before transportation begins, the labor of their production is over, and the mere fact that they were intended for interstate commerce transportation does not make their production subject to federal control under the commerce clause. . . .

Over interstate transportation, or its incidents, the regulatory power of Congress is ample, but the production of articles, intended for interstate commerce, is a matter of local regulation. . . .

It is further contended that the authority of Congress may be exerted to control interstate commerce in the shipment of child-made goods because of the effect of the circulation of such goods in other States where the evil of this class of labor has been recognized by local legislation, and the right to thus employ child labor has been more rigorously restrained than in the State of production. In other words, that the unfair competition, thus engendered, may be controlled by closing the channels of interstate commerce to manufacturers in those States where the local laws do not meet what Congress deems to be the more just standard of other States.

There is no power vested in Congress to require the States to exercise their police power so as to prevent possible unfair competition. Many causes may cooperate to give one State, by reason of local laws or conditions, an economic advantage over others. The Commerce Clause was not intended to give to Congress a general authority to equalize such conditions. In some of the States laws have been passed fixing minimum wages for women, in others the local law regulates the hours of labor of women in various employments. Business done in such States may be at an economic disadvantage when compared with States which have no such regulations; surely, this fact does not give Congress the power to deny transportation in interstate commerce to those who carry on business where the hours of labor and the rate of compensation for women have not been fixed by a standard in use in other States and approved by Congress.

The grant of power to Congress over the subject of interstate commerce was to enable it to regulate such commerce, and not to give it authority to control the States in the exercise of the police power over local trade and manufacture.

The grant of authority over a purely federal matter was not intended to destroy the local power always existing and carefully reserved to the States in the Tenth Amendment to the Constitution. . . .

We have neither authority nor disposition to question the motives of Congress in enacting this legislation. The purposes intended must be attained consistently with constitutional limitations and not by an invasion of the powers of the States. This court has no more important function than that which devolves upon it the obligation to preserve inviolate the constitutional limitations upon the exercise of authority, federal and state, to the end that each may continue to discharge harmoniously with the other, the duties entrusted to it by the Constitution.

In our view the necessary effect of this act is, by means of a prohibition against the movement in interstate commerce of ordinary commercial commodities, to regulate the hours of labor of children in factories and mines within the States, a purely state authority. Thus the act in a twofold sense is repugnant to the Constitution. It not only transcends the authority delegated to Congress over commerce but also exerts a power as to a purely local matter to which the federal authority does not extend. The far reaching result of upholding the act cannot be more plainly indicated than by pointing out that if Congress can thus regulate matters entrusted to local authority by prohibition of the movement of commodities in interstate commerce, all freedom of commerce will be at an end, and the power of the States over local matters may be eliminated, and thus our system of government be practically destroyed.

For these reasons we hold that this law exceeds the constitutional authority of Congress. . . .

[Mr. Justice Holmes, dissenting] . . . . If there is any matter upon which civilized countries have agreed—far more unanimously than they have with regard to intoxicants and some other matters over which this country is now emotionally aroused—it is the evil of premature and excessive child labor. I should have thought that if we were to introduce our own moral conceptions where in my opinion they do not belong, this was pre-eminently a case for upholding the exercise of all its powers by the United States.

But I had thought that the propriety of the exercise of a power admitted to exist in some cases for the consideration of Congress alone and that this Court always had disavowed the right to intrude its judgment upon questions of policy or morals. It is not for this Court to pronounce when prohibition is necessary to regulation if it ever may be necessary—to say that it is permissible as against strong drink but not as against the product of ruined lives.

— 22 —

SCHENCK v. UNITED STATES

249 U.S. 47 (1919)

The Schenck case is important today primarily because it provided the first statement from the Supreme Court of the "clear and present danger doctrine," a doctrine which in recent years has been the subject of much controversy as the Court has attempted in varying situations to draw a line between constitutional grants of power and constitutional prohibitions. As one of the few important decisions of the period of World War I, it dealt with the restrictions of the Espionage Act as they bore upon the freedoms of speech and press guaranteed by the First Amendment. For evidence of present-day confusion over the famous doctrine there announced, see Dennis *v.* United States, *341 U.S. 494 (1951), where justices differ not only over the interpretation of the doctrine but also over whether the validity of the exercise of power to inhibit Communist activities depends on existence of a clear and present danger.*

ｆ   ｆ   ｆ

[Mr. Justice Holmes] . . . . This is an indictment in three counts. The first charges a conspiracy to violate the Espionage Act of June 15, 1917 . . . by causing and attempting to cause insubordination, &c., in the military and naval forces of the United States, and to obstruct the recruiting and enlistment service of the United States, when the United States was at war with the German Empire, to-wit, that the defendant wilfully conspired to have printed and circulated to men who had been called and accepted for military service under the Act of May 18, 1917, a document set forth and alleged to be calculated to cause such insubordination and obstruction. The count alleges overt acts in pursuance of the conspiracy, ending in the distribution of the document set forth. The second count alleges a conspiracy to commit an offense against the United States to-wit, to use the mails for the transmission of matter declared to be non-mailable by . . . the Act of June 15, 1917, to-wit, the above mentioned document, with an averment of the same overt acts. The third count charges an unlawful use of the mails for the transmission of the same matter and otherwise as above. The defendants were found guilty on all the counts. They set up the First Amendment to the Constitution forbidding Congress to make any law abridging the freedom of speech, or of the press, and bringing the case here on that ground have argued some other points also of which we must dispose.

It is argued that the evidence, if admissible, was not sufficient to prove that the defendant Schenck was concerned in sending the documents. According to the testimony Schenck said he was general secretary of the Socialist party and had charge of the Socialist headquarters from which the documents were sent. He identified a book found there as the minutes of the Executive Committee of the party. The book showed a resolution of August 13, 1917, that 15,000 leaflets should be printed on the other side of one of them in use, to be mailed to men who had passed exemption boards, and for distribution. Schenck personally attended to the printing. On August 20 the general secretary's report said, "Obtained new leaflets from printer and started work addressing envelopes," etc.; and there was a resolve that Comrade Schenck be allowed $125 for sending leaflets through the mail. He said that he had about fifteen or sixteen thousand printed. There were files of the circular in question in the inner office which he said were printed on the other side of the one sided circular and were there for distribution. Other copies were proved to have been sent through the mails to drafted men. Without going into confirmatory details that were proved, no reasonable man could doubt that the defendant Schenck was largely instrumental in sending the circulars about. As to the defendant Baer there was evidence that she was a member of the Executive Board and that the minutes of its transactions were hers. The argument as to the sufficiency of the evidence that the defendants conspired to send the documents only impairs the seriousness of the real defense. . . .

The document in question upon its first printed side recited the first section of the Thirteenth Amendment, said that the idea embodied in it was violated by the Conscription Act and that a conscript is little better than a convict. In impassioned language it intimated that conscription was despotism in its worst form and a monstrous wrong against humanity in the interest of Wall Street's chosen few. It said, "Do not submit to intimidation," but in form at least confined itself to peaceful measures such as a petition for the repeal of the act. The other and later printed side of the sheet was headed "Assert Your Rights." It stated reasons for alleging that anyone violated the Constitution when he refused to recognize "your right to assert opposition to the draft,"

and went on, "If you do not assert and support your
rights, you are helping to deny or disparage rights which
it is the solemn duty of all citizens and residents of the
United States to retain." It described the arguments on
the other side as coming from cunning politicians and a
mercenary capitalist press, and even silent consent to
the conscription law as helping to support an infamous
conspiracy. It denied the power to send our citizens away
to foreign shores to shoot up the people of other lands,
and added that words could not express the condemnation such cold-blooded ruthlessness deserves, . . . wind-
ing up, "You must do your share to maintain, support
and uphold the rights of the people of this country." Of
course the document would not have been sent unless
it had been intended to have some effect, and we do not
see what effect it could be expected to have upon persons subject to the draft except to influence them to
obstruct the carrying of it out. The defendants do not
deny that the jury might find against them on this point.

But it is said, suppose that that was the tendency of
this circular, it is protected by the First Amendment to
the Constitution. Two of the strongest expressions are
said to be quoted respectively from well-known public
men. It well may be that the prohibition of laws abridging the freedom of speech is not confined to previous
restraints, although to prevent them may have been the
main purpose, as intimated in Paterson v. Colorado, 205
U.S. 454, 462. We admit that in many places and in
ordinary times the defendants in saying all that was said
in the circular would have been within their constitutional rights. But the character of every act depends
upon the circumstances in which it is done. . . . The
most stringent protection of free speech would not protect a man in falsely shouting fire in a theatre and
causing a panic. It does not even protect a man from
an injunction against uttering words that may have all
the effect of force. . . . The question in every case is
whether the words are used in such circumstances and
are of such a nature as to create a clear and present danger that they will bring about the substantive evils that
Congress has a right to prevent. It is a question of prox-
imity and degree. When a nation is at war many things
that might be said in time of peace are such a hindrance

to its effort that their utterance will not be endured so long as men fight and that no court could regard them as protected by any constitutional right. It seems to be admitted that if an actual obstruction of the recruiting service were proved, liability for words that produced that effect might be enforced. The statute of 1917 . . . punishes conspiracies to obstruct as well as actual obstruction. If the act (speaking, or circulating a paper), its tendency and the intent with which it is done, are the same, we perceive no ground for saying that success alone warrants making the act a crime. Goldman v. United States, 245 U.S. 474, 477. Indeed that case might be said to dispose of the present contention if the precedent covers all *media concludendi*. But as the right to free speech was not referred to specifically, we have thought fit to add a few words. . . .

— 23 —

ADKINS v. CHILDREN'S HOSPITAL

261 U.S. 525 (1923)

During the nearly two decades which followed the decision in the Lochner case (see Document No. 20) *in 1905, the Supreme Court seemed to move away from the extreme laissez faire position taken in that case. It allowed a wider range of exercise of state police power, particularly as far as the regulation of hours of labor was concerned. Even where wages and prices were involved, the Court permitted regulation in emergency situations, as in* Wilson v. New, *243 U.S. 332 (1917) and* Block v. Hirsh, *256 U.S. 135 (1921). But in the Adkins case, here presented, which was decided in 1923 amid a resurgence of conservatism on the Court and*

*throughout the country, the Court blocked a growing
movement on the part of the federal government as well
as of the states to fix minimum wages for which people
might be employed. The statute here involved was an
act of Congress for the government of the District of
Columbia. A hospital which employed workers at less
than the minimum wages set, and a hotel elevator op-
erator who lost her job because of the unwillingness of
the hotel to pay the amount of the minimum wage,
challenged the statute as a violation of due process rights.
In a dissenting opinion, Chief Justice Taft expressed the
belief that the Lochner case had been overruled* sub
silentio, *but the majority stressed the fact that the principles of that case had never been disapproved. The
Adkins decision, although arousing widespread protest,
provided the measure of constitutional rights in this field
until it was overruled in* West Coast Hotel Co. v. Par-
rish, 300 U.S. 379 (1937), *as a part of the redirection
of trend in decisions which came during the New Deal
period when Congress was weighing President Roosevelt's plan to pack the Court with new members.*

✓   ✓   ✓

[Mr. Justice Sutherland] . . . . The statute now under
consideration is attacked upon the ground that it authorizes an unconstitutional interference with the freedom of contract included within the guaranties of the
due process clause of the Fifth Amendment. That the
right to contract about one's affairs is a part of the liberty
of the individual protected by this clause is settled by the
decisions of this Court and is no longer open to question. . . . Within this liberty are contracts of employment of labor. In making such contracts, generally speaking, the parties have an equal right to obtain from each
other the best terms they can as the result of private
bargaining. . . .

There is, of course, no such thing as absolute freedom
of contract. It is subject to a great variety of restraints.
But freedom of contract is, nevertheless, the general
rule and restraint the exception; and the exercise of legislative authority to abridge it can be justified only by the
existence of exceptional circumstances. Whether these

circumstances exist in the present case constitute the question to be answered. It will be helpful to this end to review some of the decisions where the interference has been upheld and consider the grounds upon which they rest.

(1) Those dealing with statutes fixing rates and charges to be exacted by businesses impressed with a public interest. . . . This class of cases may be laid aside as inapplicable.

(2) Statutes relating to contracts for the performance of public work. . . . We may . . . dismiss these decisions from consideration as inapplicable.

(3) Statutes prescribing the character, methods and time for payment of wages. . . . In no sense can they be said to be, or to furnish a precedent for, wage-fixing statutes.

(4) Statutes fixing hours of labor. It is upon this class that the greatest emphasis is laid in argument and therefore, and because such cases approach most nearly the line of principle applicable to the statute here involved, we shall consider them more at length. . . .

If now, in the light furnished by the foregoing exceptions to the general rule forbidding legislative interference with freedom of contract, we examine and analyze the statute in question, we shall see that it differs from them in every material respect. It is not a law dealing with any business charged with a public interest, or with public work, or to meet and tide over a temporary emergency. It has nothing to do with the character, methods or periods of wage payments. It does not prescribe hours of labor or conditions under which labor is to be done. It is not for the protection of persons under legal disability or for the prevention of fraud. It is simply and exclusively a price-fixing law, confined to adult women (for we are not now considering the provisions relating to minors), who are legally as capable of contracting for themselves as men. It forbids two parties having lawful capacity—under penalties as to the employer—to freely contract with one another in respect of the price for which one shall render service to the other in a purely private employment where both are willing, perhaps anxious, to agree, even though the consequences may be to oblige one to surrender a desirable employment and the other to dispense with the services of a desirable employee. . . .

The standard furnished by the statute for the guidance of the board is so vague as to be impossible of practical application with any reasonable degree of accuracy. What is sufficient to supply the necessary cost of living for a woman worker and maintain her in good health and protect her morals is obviously not a precise or unvarying sum—not even approximately so. The amount will depend upon a variety of circumstances; the individual temperament, habits of thrift, care, ability to buy necessaries intelligently, and whether the woman lives alone or with her family. To those who practice economy, a given sum will afford comfort, while to those of contrary habit the same sum will be wholly inadequate. The cooperative economies of the family group are not taken into account though they constitute an important consideration in estimating the cost of living, for it is obvious that the individual expense will be less in the case of a member of a family than in the case of one living alone. The relation between earnings and morals is not capable of standardization. It cannot be shown that well-paid women safeguard their morals more carefully than those who are poorly paid. Morality rests upon other considerations than wages; and there is, certainly, no such prevalent connection between the two as to justify a broad attempt to adjust the latter with reference to the former. As a means of safeguarding morals the attempted classification, in our opinion, is without reasonable basis. No distinction can be made between women who work for others and those who do not; nor is there ground for distinction between women and men, for, certainly, if women require a minimum wage to preserve their morals men require it to preserve their honesty. For these reasons, and others which might be stated, the inquiry in respect of the necessary cost of living and of the income necessary to preserve health and morals, presents an individual and not a composite question, and must be answered for each individual considered by herself and not by a general formula prescribed by a statutory bureau. . . .

The feature of this statute which, perhaps more than any other, puts upon it the stamp of invalidity is that it exacts from the employer an arbitrary payment for a purpose and upon a basis having no causal connection with his business, or the contract or the work the employee engages to do. The declared basis, as already pointed out, is not the value of the service rendered, but the extraneous circumstance that the employee needs to get a prescribed sum of money to insure her subsistence, health and morals. The ethical right of every worker, man or woman, to a living wage may be conceded. One of the declared and important purposes of trade organizations is to secure it. And with that principle and with every legitimate effort to realize it in fact, no one can quarrel; but the fallacy of the proposed method of attaining it is that it assumes that every employer is bound at all events to furnish it. The moral requirement implicit in every contract of employment, viz., that the amount to be paid and the service to be rendered shall bear to each other some relation of just equivalence, is completely ignored. The necessities of the employee are alone considered and these arise outside of the employment, are the same when there is no employment, and as great in one occupation as in another. Certainly the employer by paying a fair equivalent for the service rendered, though not sufficient to support the employee, has neither caused nor contributed to her poverty. On the contrary, to the extent of what he pays he has relieved it. In principle, there can be no difference between the case of selling labor and the case of selling goods. If one goes to the butcher, the baker or grocer to buy food, he is morally entitled to obtain the worth of his money but he is not entitled to more. If what he gets is worth what he pays he is not justified in demanding more simply because he needs more; and the shopkeeper, having dealt fairly and honestly in that transaction, is not concerned in any peculiar sense with the question of his customer's necessities. Should a statute undertake to vest in a commission power to determine the quantity of food necessary for individual support and require the shopkeeper, if he sells to the individual at all, to furnish that quantity at not more than a fixed maximum, it would undoubtedly fall before the constitutional test. The fallacy of any argument in support of the validity of such a statute would be quickly exposed. The argument in support of that now being considered is equally fallacious, though the weakness of it may not be so plain. A statute requiring an employer to pay in money, to pay at prescribed and regular intervals, to pay the value of services rendered, even to pay with fair relation to the extent of the benefit obtained from the service, would be understandable. But a statute which prescribes payment without regard to any of these things and solely with relation to circumstances apart from the contract of employment, the business affected by it and the work done under it, is so clearly the product of a naked, arbitrary exercise of power that it cannot be allowed to stand under the Constitution of the United States. . . .

It follows from what has been said that the act in question passes the limit prescribed by the Constitution, and, accordingly, the decrees of the court below are affirmed.

[Mr. Justice Holmes, dissenting] . . . . I confess that I do not understand the principle on which the power to fix a minimum for the wages of women can be denied by those who admit the power to fix a maximum for their hours of work. I fully assent to the proposition that here as elsewhere the distinctions of the law are distinctions of degree, but I perceive no difference in the kind or degree of interference with liberty, the only matter with which we have any concern, between the one case and the other. The bargain is equally affected whichever half you regulate. . . .

The criterion of constitutionality is not whether we believe the law to be for the public good. We certainly cannot be prepared to deny that a reasonable man reasonably might have that belief in view of the legislation of Great Britain, Victoria and a number of the States of this Union. The belief is fortified by a very remarkable collection of documents submitted on behalf of the appellants, material here, I conceive, only as showing that the belief reasonably may be held. . . .

I am of opinion that the statute is valid and that the decree should be reversed.

— 24 —

MYERS v. UNITED STATES

272 U.S. 52 (1926)

Since the time when the federal government was organized there had been dispute over the extent of the power of the President over officers who had been appointed by him with the advice and consent of the Senate. Believers in a strong executive contended that since the executive power was vested in the President he could remove at will any person appointed to serve under him, without the intervention of the Senate in the removal process. Men concerned about maintenance of an effective balance of power among the branches of the government contended, however, that Congress could make removal from administrative office conditional upon the consent of the Senate. The issue had been involved in the impeachment of Andrew Johnson, who in violation of the Tenure of Office Act had removed Secretary of War Edwin M. Stanton without securing senatorial consent, but no Supreme Court determination of the question was there involved.

The issue reached the Court as a result of the action of President Woodrow Wilson, in 1920, in removing Frank S. Myers, a first-class postmaster, before the end of his term without securing senatorial permission as required by statute. Myers challenged the removal by bringing suit for salary beyond the date of removal. Losing in the Court of Claims, Myers appealed to the Supreme Court where his case was argued twice, was much discussed among members of the Court, and was pending almost two years before it was finally decided. The Court held by a vote of six to three that Congress could not limit the President's power to remove executive officers. The majority opinion was written by Chief Justice Taft, who as an ex-President knew well the difficulty of maintaining presidential control over executive em-

ployees without the power of removal at will. In Humphrey's Executor v. United States, 295 U.S. 602 (1935), *the Supreme Court later restricted the Myers opinion in so far as it dealt with officers of quasi-legislative and quasi-judicial agencies, but as to administrative officers the Myers decision still holds, to the effect that the President can remove them in spite of any obstructions which Congress may attempt to set up.*

✓   ✓   ✓

[Mr. Chief Justice Taft] . . . . The relevant parts of article 2 of the Constitution are as follows:

"Section 1. The executive power shall be vested in a President of the United States of America. . . ."

The vesting of the executive power in the President was essentially a grant of the power to execute the laws. But the President alone and unaided could not execute the laws. He must execute them by the assistance of subordinates. . . . As he is charged specifically to take care that they be faithfully executed, the reasonable implication, even in the absence of express words, was that as part of his executive power he should select those who were to act for him under his direction in the execution of the laws. The further implication must be, in the absence of any express limitation respecting removals, that as his selection of administrative officers is essential to the execution of the laws by him, so must be his power of removing those for whom he cannot continue to be responsible. . . .

The view of Mr. Madison and his associates was that not only did the grant of executive power to the President in the first section of article 2 carry with it the power of removal, but the express recognition of the power of appointment in the second section enforced this view on the well-approved principle of constitutional and statutory construction that the power of removal of executive officers was incident to the power of appointment. . . . This principle as a rule of constitutional and statutory construction, then generally conceded, has been recognized ever since. . . . The reason for the principle is that those in charge of and responsible for administering functions of government, who select their executive subordinates, need in meeting their responsibility to have the power to remove those whom they appoint.

Under section 2 of article 2, however, the power of appointment by the executive is restricted in its exercise by the provision that the Senate, a part of the legislative branch of the government, may check the action of the executive by rejecting the officers he selects. Does this make the Senate part of the removing power? . . .

The history of the clause by which the Senate was given a check upon the President's power of appointment makes it clear that it was not prompted by any desire to limit removals. As already pointed out, the important purpose of those who brought about the restriction was to lodge in the Senate, where the small states had equal representation with the larger states, power to prevent the President from making too many appointments from the larger states. . . .

A veto by the Senate—a part of the legislative branch of the government—upon removals is a much greater limitation upon the executive branch, and a much more serious blending of the legislative with the executive, than a rejection of a proposed appointment. It is not to be implied. The rejection of a nominee of the President for a particular office does not greatly embarrass him in the conscientious discharge of his high duties in the selection of those who are to aid him, because the President usually has an ample field from which to select for office, according to his preference, competent and capable men. . . .

The power to prevent the removal of an officer who has served under the President is different from the authority to consent to or reject his appointment. When a nomination is made, it may be presumed that the Senate is, or may become, as well advised as to the fitness of the nominee as the President, but in the nature of things the defects in ability or intelligence or loyalty in the administration of the laws of one who has served as an officer under the President are facts as to which the President, or his trusted subordinates, must be better informed than the Senate, and the power to remove him may, therefore, be regarded as confined for very sound and practical reasons, to the governmental authority which has administrative control. The power of removal is incident to the power of appointment, not to the power of advising and consenting to appointment, and when the grant of the executive power is enforced by the express mandate to take care that the laws be faithfully executed, it emphasizes the necessity for including within the executive power as conferred the exclusive power of removal. . . .

Made responsible under the Constitution for the effective enforcement of the law, the President needs as an indispensable aid to meet it the disciplinary influence upon those who act under him of a reserve power of removal. . . . The degree of guidance in the discharge of their duties that the President may exercise over executive officers varies with the character of their service as prescribed in the law under which they act. The highest and most important duties which his subordinates perform are those in which they act for him. In such cases they are exercising not their own but his discretion. This field is a very large one. It is sometimes described as political. . . . Each head of a department is and must be the President's alter ego in the matters of that department where the President is required by law to exercise authority. . . .

In all such cases, the discretion to be exercised is that of the President in determining the national public interest and in directing the action to be taken by his executive subordinates to protect it. In this field his cabinet officers must do his will. He must place in each member of his official family, and his chief executive subordinates, implicit faith. The moment that he loses confidence in the intelligence, ability, judgment, or loyalty of any one of them, he must have the power to remove him without delay. To require him to file charges and submit them to the consideration of the Senate might make impossible that unity and co-ordination in executive administration essential to effective action. . . .

But this is not to say there are not strong reasons why the President should have a like power to remove his appointees charged with other duties than those above described. The ordinary duties of officers prescribed by statute come under the general administrative control of the President by virtue of the general grant to him of the executive power, and he may properly supervise and guide their construction of the statutes under which they act in order to secure that unitary and uniform execution of the laws which article 2 of the Constitution evidently contemplated in vesting general executive power in the President alone. Laws are often passed with specific provision for the adoption of regulations by a department or bureau head to make the law workable and effective. The ability and judgment manifested by the official thus empowered, as well as his energy and stimulation of his subordinates, are subjects which the President must consider and supervise in his administrative control. Finding such officers to be negligent and inefficient, the President should have the power to remove them. Of course there may be duties so peculiarly and specifically committed to the discretion of a particular officer as to raise a question whether the President may overrule or revise the officer's interpretation of his statutory duty in a particular instance. Then there may be duties of a quasi judicial character imposed on executive officers and members of executive tribunals whose decisions after hearing affect interests of individuals, the discharge of which the President cannot in a particular case properly influence or control. But even in such a case he may consider the decision after its rendition as a reason for removing the officer, on the ground that the discretion regularly entrusted to that officer by statute has not been on the whole intelligently or wisely exercised. Otherwise he does not discharge his own constitutional duty of seeing that the laws be faithfully executed. . . .

What, then, are the elements that enter into our decision of this case? We have, first, a construction of the Constitution made by a Congress which was to provide by legislation for the organization of the government in accord with the Constitution which had just then been adopted, and in which there was, as Representatives and Senators, a considerable number of those who had been members of the convention that framed the Constitution and presented it for ratification. . . . This construction was followed by the legislative department and the executive department continuously for 73 years, and this, although the matter in the heat of political differences between the executive and the Senate in President Jack-

son's time, was the subject of bitter controversy, as we
have seen. This court has repeatedly laid down the principle that a contemporaneous legislative exposition of
the Constitution, when the founders of our government
and framers of our Constitution were actively participating in public affairs, acquiesced in for a long term of
years, fixes the construction to be given its provisions. . . .

We are now asked to set aside this construction thus
buttressed and adopt an adverse view, because the Congress of the United States did so during a heated political difference of opinion between the then President and
the majority leaders of Congress over the reconstruction
measures adopted as a means of restoring to their proper
status the states which attempted to withdraw from the
Union at the time of the Civil War. The extremes to
which the majority in both Houses carried legislative
measures in that matter are now recognized by all who
calmly review the history of the episode in our government leading to articles of impeachment against President Johnson and his acquittal. Without animadverting
on the character of the measures taken, we are certainly
justified in saying that they should not be given the
weight affecting proper constitutional construction to be
accorded to that reached by the First Congress of the
United States during a political calm and acquiesced in
by the whole government for three-quarters of a century,
especially when the new construction contended for has
never been acquiesced in by either the executive or the
judicial departments. While this court has studiously
avoided deciding the issue until it was presented in such
a way that could not be avoided, in the references it has
made to the history of the question, and in the presump-
tions it has indulged in favor of a statutory construction
not inconsistent with the legislative decision of 1789, it
has indicated a trend of view that we should not and cannot ignore. When on the merits we find our conclusion
strongly favoring the view which prevailed in the First
Congress, we have no hesitation in holding that conclusion to be correct; and it therefore follows that the
Tenure of Office Act of 1867, in so far as it attempted
to prevent the President from removing executive officers
who had been appointed by him by and with the advice

and consent of the Senate, was invalid and that subsequent legislation of the same effect was equally so.

For the reasons given, we must therefore hold that the provision of the law of 1876 by which the unrestricted power of removal of first-class postmasters is denied to the President is in violation of the Constitution and invalid. This leads to an affirmance of the judgment of the Court of Claims.

— 25 —

HOME BUILDING &
LOAN ASSOCIATION
v. BLAISDELL

290 U.S. 398 (1934)

In many parts of the country the depression of the early 1930's brought chaos to property relationships. In the field of real estate, debtors found themselves unable to pay their debts, with the result that wholesale foreclosures on mortgages took place. Yet such foreclosures only drove lower the already declining value of property, indicating that the foreclosure process proved destructive for "land poor" creditors as well as for debtors. In a similar situation a century earlier stemming from the panic of 1837 the Supreme Court, in Bronson v. Kinzie, *1 Howard 311 (1843), had held unconstitutional an Illinois statute postponing foreclosure and forbidding sale of property for less than two-thirds of the appraised value of the property. Such action, said the Court, impaired the obligation of contracts.*

In 1933, however, the State of Minnesota enacted a similar statute, though one limited to the period of the emergency and giving somewhat more protection to the rights of creditors than had been involved in the Illinois

*statute. The case reached the Supreme Court when the
country was in the trough of the depression and just as
the New Deal program of the federal government was
getting under way. The Supreme Court, dividing five to
four, upheld the Minnesota statute in the light of the
economic situation which the emergency had produced.
The decision brought an important discussion of the nature of emergency power and the relation of emergencies
to the dimensions of constitutional powers and constitutional rights. The case merits attention both for the legal
issues and for its portrayal of an important segment of
our history.*

⟋   ⟋   ⟋

[Mr. Chief Justice Hughes] . . . . The state court upheld the statute as an emergency measure. Although con-
ceding that the obligations of the mortgage contract were
impaired, the court decided that what it thus described
as an impairment was, notwithstanding the contract
clause of the Federal Constitution, within the police
power of the state as that power was called into exercise
by the public economic emergency which the Legislature
had found to exist. Attention is thus directed to the
preamble and first section of the statute which described
the existing emergency in terms that were deemed to
justify the temporary relief which the statute affords. The
state court, declaring that it could not say that this legislative finding was without basis, supplemented that finding by its own statement of conditions of which it took
judicial notice. The court said:

"In addition to the weight to be given the determination of the Legislature that an economic emergency
exists which demands relief, the court must take notice
of other considerations. The members of the Legislature
come from every community of the state and from all
walks of life. They are familiar with conditions generally
in every calling, occupation, profession, and business in
the state. Not only they, but the courts must be guided
by what is common knowledge. It is common knowledge
that in the last few years land values have shrunk enor-
mously. Loans made a few years ago upon the basis of
the then going values cannot possibly be replaced on the

basis of present values. We all know that when this law was enacted the large financial companies, which had made it their business to invest in mortgages, had ceased to do so. No bank would directly or indirectly loan on real estate mortgages. Life insurance companies, large investors on such mortgages, had even declared a moratorium as to the loan provisions of their policy contracts. The President had closed banks temporarily. The Congress, in addition to many extraordinary measures looking to the relief of the economic emergency, had passed an act to supply funds whereby mortgagors may be able within a reasonable time to refinance their mortgages or redeem from sales where the redemption has not expired. With this knowledge the court cannot well hold that the Legislature had no basis in fact for the conclusion that an economic emergency existed which called for the exercise of the police power to grant relief." . . .

In determining whether the provision for this temporary and conditional relief exceeds the power of the state by reason of the clause of the Federal Constitution prohibiting impairment of the obligations of contracts, we must consider the relation of emergency to constitutional power, the historical setting of the contract clause, the development of the jurisprudence of this Court in the construction of that clause, and the principles of construction which we may consider to be established.

Emergency does not create power. Emergency does not increase granted power or remove or diminish the restrictions imposed upon power granted or reserved. The Constitution was adopted in a period of grave emergency. Its grants of power to the federal government and its limitations of the power of the States were determined in the light of emergency, and they are not altered by emergency. What power was thus granted and what limitations were thus imposed are questions which have always been, and always will be, the subject of close examination under our constitutional system.

While emergency does not create power, emergency may furnish the occasion for the exercise of power. "Although an emergency may not call into life a power which has never lived, nevertheless emergency may afford a reason for the exertion of a living power already enjoyed." Wilson v. New, 243 U.S. 332, 348. The constitutional question presented in the light of an emergency is whether the power possessed embraces the particular exercise of it in response to particular conditions. Thus, the war power of the federal government is not created by the emergency of war, but it is a power given to meet that emergency. It is a power to wage war successfully, and thus it permits the harnessing of the entire energies of the people in a supreme co-operative effort to preserve the nation. But even the war power does not remove constitutional limitations safeguarding essential liberties. When the provisions of the Constitution, in grant or restriction, are specific, so particularized, as not to admit of construction, no question is presented. . . . But, where constitutional grants and limitations of power are set forth in general clauses, which afford a broad outline, the process of construction is essential to fill in the details. That is true of the contract clause. . . .

But full recognition of the occasion and general purpose of the clause does not suffice to fix its precise scope. Nor does an examination of the details of prior legislation in the States yield criteria which can be considered controlling. To ascertain the scope of the constitutional prohibition, we examine the course of judicial decisions in its application. These put it beyond question that the prohibition is not an absolute one and is not to be read with literal exactness like a mathematical formula. . . .

The inescapable problems of construction have been: What is a contract? What are the obligations of contract? What constitutes impairment of these obligations? What residuum of power is there still in the States, in relation to the operation of contracts, to protect the vital interests of the community? Questions of this character, "of no small nicety and intricacy, have vexed the legislative halls, as well as the judicial tribunals, with an uncounted variety and frequency of litigation and speculation." Story on the Constitution, Section 1375.

The obligation of a contract is the law which binds the parties to perform their agreement. . . . This Court has said that "the laws which subsist at the time and place of the making of a contract, and where it is to be performed, enter into and form a part of it, as if they were expressly referred to or incorporated in its terms. This principle embraces alike those which affect its validity, construction, discharge, and enforcement. . . . Nothing can be more material to the obligation than the means of enforcement. . . . The ideas of validity and remedy are inseparable, and both are parts of the obligation, which is guaranteed by the Constitution against invasion." Von Hoffman v. City of Quincy, 4 Wall. 535, 550, 552. . . . But this broad language cannot be taken without qualification. Chief Justice Marshall pointed out the distinction between obligation and remedy. Sturges v. Crowinshield, supra, 4 Wheat. 200. Said he: "The distinction between the obligation of a contract, and the remedy given by the legislature to enforce that obligation, has been taken at the bar, and exists in the nature of things. Without impairing the obligation of the contract, the remedy may certainly be modified as the wisdom of the nation shall direct." And in Von Hoffman v. City of Quincy, 4 Wall. 553, 554, the general statement above quoted was limited by the further observation that "it is competent for the States to change the form of the remedy, or to modify it otherwise, as they may see fit, provided no substantial right secured by the contract is thereby impaired. No attempt has been made to fix definitely the line between alterations of the remedy, which are to be deemed legitimate, and those which, under the form of modifying the remedy, impair substantial rights. Every case must be determined upon its own circumstances." And Chief Justice Waite, quoting this language in Antoni v. Greenhow, 107 U.S. 769, 775, added: "In all such cases the question becomes, therefore, one of reasonableness, and of that the legislature is primarily the judge." . . .

Not only is the constitutional provision qualified by the measure of control which the state retains over remedial processes, but the state also continues to possess authority to safeguard the vital interests of its people. It does not matter that legislation appropriate to that end "has the result of modifying or abrogating contracts already in effect." Stephenson v. Binford, 287 U.S. 251, 276. Not only are existing laws read into contracts in order to fix obligations as between the parties, but the reservation of essential attributes of sovereign power is also read into contracts as a postulate of the legal order.

The policy of protecting contracts against impairment presupposes the maintenance of a government by virtue of which contractual relations are worth while,—a government which retains adequate authority to secure the peace and good order of society. This principle of harmonizing the constitutional prohibition with the necessary residuum of state power has had progressive recognition in the decisions of this Court. . . .

Undoubtedly, whatever is reserved of state power must be consistent with the fair intent of the constitutional limitation of that power. The reserved power cannot be construed so as to destroy the limitation, nor is the limitation to be construed to destroy the reserved power in its essential aspects. They must be construed in harmony with each other. This principle precludes a construction which would permit the state to adopt as its policy the repudiation of debts or the destruction of contracts or the denial of means to enforce them. But it does not follow that conditions may not arise in which a temporary restraint of enforcement may not be consistent with the spirit and purpose of the constitutional provision and thus be found to be within the range of the reserved power of the state to protect the vital interests of the community. It cannot be maintained that the constitutional prohibition should be so construed as to prevent limited and temporary interpositions with respect to the enforcement of contracts if made necessary by a great public calamity such as fire, flood, or earthquake. . . . The reservation of state power appropriate to such extraordinary conditions may be deemed to be as much a part of all contracts as is the reservation of state power to protect the public interest in the other situations to which we have referred. And, if state power exists to give temporary relief from the enforcement of contracts in the presence of disasters due to physical causes such as fire, flood, or earthquake, that power cannot be said to be nonexistent when the urgent public need demanding such relief is produced by other and economic causes. . . .

Whatever doubt there may have been that the protective power of the state, its police power, may be exercised—without violating the true intent of the provision of the Federal Constitution—in directly preventing the immediate and literal enforcement of contractual obligations by a temporary and conditional restraint, where vital public interests would otherwise suffer, was removed by our decisions relating to the enforcement of provisions of leases during a period of scarcity of housing. . . .

It is manifest from this review of our decisions that there has been a growing appreciation of public needs and of the necessity of finding ground for a rational compromise between individual rights and public welfare. The settlement and consequent contraction of the public domain, the pressure of a constantly increasing density of population, the inter-relation of the activities of our people and the complexity of our economic interests, have inevitably led to an increased use of the organization of society in order to protect the very bases of individual opportunity. Where, in earlier days, it was thought that only the concerns of individuals or of classes were involved, and that those of the state itself were touched only remotely, it has later been found that the fundamental interests of the state are directly affected; and that the question is no longer merely that of one party to a contract as against another, but of the use of reasonable means to safeguard the economic structure upon which the goods of all depends. . . .

Nor is it helpful to attempt to draw a fine distinction between the intended meaning of the words of the Constitution and their intended application. When we consider the contract clause and the decisions which have expounded it in harmony with the essential reserved power of the states to protect the security of their peoples, we find no warrant for the conclusion that the clause has been warped by these decisions from its proper significance or that the founders of our government would have interpreted the clause differently had they had occasion to assume that responsibility in the conditions of the later day. The vast body of law which has been developed was unknown to the fathers, but it is believed to have preserved the essential content and the spirit of the Constitution. With a growing recognition of public needs and the relation of individual rights to public security, the court has sought to prevent the perversion of the clause through its use as an instrument to throttle the capacity of the states to protect their fundamental interests. This development is a growth from the seeds which the fathers planted. . . . The principle of this development is, as we have seen, that the reservation of the reasonable exercise of the protective power of the state is read into all contracts, and there is no greater reason for refusing to apply this principle to Minnesota than to New York leases. . . .

We are of the opinion that the Minnesota statute as here applied does not violate the contract clause of the Federal Constitution. Whether the legislation is wise or unwise as a matter of policy is a question with which we are not concerned.

What has been said on that point is also applicable to the contention presented under the due process clause. Block v. Hirsh, supra.

Nor do we think that the statute denies to the appellant the equal protection of the laws. The classification which the statute makes cannot be said to be an arbitrary one. . . .

The judgment of the Supreme Court of Minnesota is affirmed.

— 26 —

NORMAN v. BALTIMORE & OHIO RAILROAD COMPANY

294 U.S. 240 (1935)

Among the drastic measures taken to cope with the depression of the early 1930's were those which withdrew gold from circulation as money to preserve it as backing for a currency system and, later, reduced the amount of gold used to measure the value of each dollar in circulation. The power of the government to reserve

*most of the gold in the United States primarily for mone-
tary purposes was not seriously questioned, and fixing the
weight and fineness of the specie dollar, and of the paper
dollar as well, had always been a responsibility of Congress. But Congress here took an additional step and required that existing contracts calling for payment in gold
or in dollars of the specie value that had been fixed before the devaluation should be fulfilled dollar for dollar
in specie that had the reduced gold backing. Indignant
creditors saw this requirement as an impairment of the
obligation of contracts and hence as a taking of property
without due process of law, and sought in court to compel debtors to pay additional paper dollars to make up
the amount of the devaluation in terms of the gold value
of the dollar.*

*Although the devaluation, in the neighborhood of
forty per cent, made a considerable difference in foreign
trade where gold was still used for exchange purposes, it
made little difference internally where gold had been
little used for a long time as a circulatory medium.
Prices were going up, but the rise was attributable to
various causes and not primarily to the devaluation. On
the other hand, were the courts to require the fulfillment
of existing contracts in increased amounts of paper dollars to the amount of some forty per cent, the disturbance of the economy would be tremendous. The government and thoughtful people watched anxiously the progress of cases in the courts. After cases had been argued
before the Supreme Court, that tribunal broke precedent
on certain succeeding Mondays by publicly announcing
in advance that the so-called gold-clause cases would not
be decided on those days, thereby temporarily allaying
the excitement. When a decision was finally announced,
the Court by the narrow margin of five to four upheld
the statute, leading Justice McReynolds to proclaim
orally in the court room that "As for the Constitution, it
does not seem too much to say that it is gone."*

✓   ✓   ✓

[Mr. Chief Justice Hughes] . . . . The Joint Resolution of June 5, 1933, was one of a series of measures
relating to the currency. These measures disclose not
only the purposes of the Congress but also the situations

which existed at the time the Joint Resolution was adopted and when the payments under the "gold clauses" were sought. On March 6, 1933, the President, stating that there had been "heavy and unwarranted withdrawals of gold and currency from our banking institutions for the purpose of hoarding" and "extensive speculative activity abroad in foreign exchange" which had resulted "in severe drains on the Nation's stocks of gold," and reciting the authority conferred by Section 5(b) of the Act of October 6, 1917 . . . declared "a bank holiday" until March 9, 1933. On the same date, the Secretary of the Treasury, with the President's approval, issued instruction to the Treasurer of the United States to make payments in gold in any form only under license issued by the Secretary.

On March 9, 1933, the Congress passed the Emergency Banking Act. . . . The Act also amended Section 11 of the Federal Reserve Act . . . so as to authorize the Secretary of the Treasury to require all persons to deliver to the Treasurer of the United States "any or all gold coin, gold bullion, and gold certificates" owned by them, and that the Secretary should pay therefore "an equivalent amount of any other form of coin or currency coined or issued under the laws of the United States." . . .

We have not attempted to summarize all the provisions of these measures. We are not concerned with their wisdom. The question before the Court is one of power, not of policy. And that question touches the validity of these measures at but a single point, that is, in relation to the Joint Resolution denying effect to "gold clauses" in existing contracts. The Resolution must, however, be considered in its legislative setting and in the light of other measures *in pari materia*. . . .

We are of the opinion that the gold clauses now before us were not contracts for payment in gold coin as a commodity, or in bullion, but were contracts for the payment of money. The bonds were severally for the payment of one thousand dollars. We also think that, fairly construed, these clauses were intended to afford a definite standard or measure of value, and thus to protect against a depreciation of the currency and against the discharge of the obligation by a payment of lesser value than that prescribed. When these contracts were made they were not repugnant to any action of the Congress. In order to determine whether effect may now be given to the intention of the parties in the face of the action taken by the Congress, or the contracts may be satisfied by the payment dollar for dollar, in legal tender, as the Congress has now prescribed, it is necessary to consider (1) the power of the Congress to establish a monetary system and the necessary implications of that power; (2) the power of the Congress to invalidate the provisions of existing contracts which interfere with the exercise of its constitutional authority; and (3) whether the clauses in question do constitute such an interference as to bring them within the range of that power.

Second. The power of the Congress to establish a monetary system. It is unnecessary to review the historic controversy as to the extent of this power, or again to go over the ground traversed by the Court in reaching the conclusion that the Congress may make treasury notes legal tender in payment of debts previously contracted, as well as of those subsequently contracted, whether that authority be exercised in the course of war or in time of peace. . . . We need only consider certain postulates upon which that conclusion rested.

The Constitution grants to the Congress power "To coin money, regulate the value thereof, and of foreign coin." Art. I, sec. 8, par. 5. But the Court in the legal tender cases did not derive from that express grant alone the full authority of the Congress in relation to the currency. The Court found the source of that authority in all the related powers conferred upon the Congress and appropriate to achieve "the great objects for which the government was framed,"—"a national government, with sovereign powers." . . . The broad and comprehensive national authority over the subjects of revenue, finance and currency is derived from the aggregate of the powers granted to the Congress, embracing the powers to lay and collect taxes, to borrow money, to regulate commerce with foreign nations and among the several states, to coin money, regulate the value thereof, and of foreign coin, and fix the standards of weights and measures, and the added express power "to make all laws which shall be necessary and proper for carrying into execution" the other enumerated powers. . . .

Dealing with the specific question as to the effect of the legal tender acts upon contracts made before their passage, that is, those for the payment of money generally, the Court, in the legal tender cases, recognized the possible consequences of such enactments in frustrating the expected performance of contracts,—in rendering them "fruitless or partially fruitless." . . . The conclusion was that contracts must be understood as having been made in reference to the possible exercise of the rightful authority of the Government, and that no obligation of a contract "can extend to the defeat" of that authority. . . .

On similar grounds, the Court dismissed the contention under the Fifth Amendment forbidding the taking of private property for public use without just compensation or the deprivation of it without due process of law. . . .

The question of the validity of the Joint Resolution of June 5, 1933, must be determined in the light of these settled principles.

Third. The power of the Congress to invalidate the provisions of existing contracts which interfere with the exercise of its constitutional authority. The instant cases involve contracts between private parties, but the question necessarily relates as well to the contracts or obligations of States and municipalities, or of their political subdivisions, that, is to such engagements as are within the reach of the applicable national power. The Government's own contracts—the obligations of the United States—are in a distinct category and demand separate consideration. See Perry v. United States, 294 U.S. 330.

The contention is that the power of the Congress, broadly sustained by the decisions we have cited in relation to private contracts for the payment of money generally, does not extend to the striking down of express contracts for gold payments. . . .

This argument is in the teeth of another established principle. Contracts, however express, cannot fetter the constitutional authority of the Congress. Contracts may create rights of property, but when contracts deal with a subject matter which lies within the control of the

Congress, they have a congenital infirmity. Parties cannot remove their transactions from the reach of dominant constitutional power by making contracts about them. See Hudson Water Co. v. McCarter, 209 U.S. 349, 357.

This principle has familiar illustration in the exercise of the power to regulate commerce. If shippers and carriers stipulate for specified rates, although the rates may be lawful when the contracts are made, if Congress through the Interstate Commerce Commission exercises its authority and prescribes different rates, the latter control and override inconsistent stipulations in contracts previously made. . . .

The same reasoning applies to the constitutional authority of the Congress to regulate the currency and to establish the monetary system of the country. If the gold clauses now before us interfere with the policy of the Congress in the exercise of that authority, they cannot stand.

Fourth. The effect of the gold clauses in suit in relation to the monetary policy adopted by the Congress. Despite the wide range of the discussion at the bar and the earnestness with which the arguments against the validity of the Joint Resolution have been pressed, these contentions necessarily are brought, under the dominant principles to which we have referred, to a single and narrow point. That point is whether the gold clauses do constitute an actual interference with the monetary policy of the Congress in the light of its broad power to determine that policy. Whether they may be deemed to be such an interference depends upon an appraisement of economic conditions and upon determinations of questions of fact. With respect to those conditions and determinations, the Congress is entitled to its own judgement. We may inquire whether its action is arbitrary or capricious, that is, whether it has reasonable relation to a legitimate end. If it is an appropriate means to such an end, the decision of the Congress as to the degree of the necessity for the adoption of that means, is final. . . .

The Committee on Banking and Currency of the House of Representatives stated in its report recommending favorable action upon the Joint Resolution . . .

"The occasion for the declaration in the resolution that the gold clauses are contrary to public policy arises out of the experiences of the present emergency. These gold clauses render ineffective the power of the Government to create a currency and determine the value thereof. If the gold clauses applied to a very limited number of contracts and security issues, it would be a matter of no particular consequence, but in this country virtually all obligations, almost as a matter of routine, contain the gold clause. In the light of this situation two phenomena which have developed during the present emergency make the enforcement of the gold clauses incompatible with the public interest. The first is the tendency which has developed internally to hoard gold; the second is the tendency for capital to leave the country. Under these circumstances no currency system, whether based upon gold or upon any other foundation, can meet the requirements of a situation in which many billions of dollars of securities are expressed in a particular form of the circulating medium, particularly when it is the medium upon which the entire credit and currency structure rests."

And the Joint Resolution itself recites the determination of the Congress. . . .

"Whereas the existing emergency has disclosed that provisions of obligations which purport to give the obligee a right to require payment in fold or a particular kind of coin or currency of the United States, or in an amount in money of the United States measured thereby, obstruct the power of the Congress to regulate the value of the money of the United States, and are inconsistent with the declared policy of the Congress to maintain at all times the equal power of every dollar, coined or issued by the United States, in the markets and in the payment of debts."

Can we say that this determination is so destitute of basis that the interdiction of the gold clauses must be deemed to be without any reasonable relation to the monetary policy adopted by the Congress? . . .

We are not concerned with consequences, in the sense that consequences, however serious, may excuse an invasion of constitutional right. We are concerned with the constitutional power of the Congress over the monetary system of the country and its attempted frustration. Exercising that power, the Congress has undertaken to

establish a uniform currency, and parity between kinds of
currency, and to make that currency, dollar for dollar,
legal tender for the payment of debts. In the light of
abundant experience, the Congress was entitled to choose
such a uniform system, and to reject a dual system, with
respect to all obligations within the range of the exercise
of its constitutional authority. The contention that these
gold clauses are valid contracts and cannot be struck
down proceeds upon the assumption that private parties,
and States and municipalities, may make and enforce
contracts which may limit that authority. Dismissing
that untenable assumption, the facts must be faced. We
think that it is clearly shown that these clauses interfere
with the exertion of the power granted to the Congress
and certainly it is not established that the Congress ar-
bitrarily or capriciously decided that such an interference
existed.

— 27 —

SCHECHTER POULTRY CORPORATION v. UNITED STATES

295 U.S. 495 (1935)

*The National Industrial Recovery Act of 1933 was
enacted as one of the measures calculated to lift the country out of the business depression and restore prosperity.
It provided for the establishment of codes of fair competition which were intended to eliminate the excesses
of competition which were believed to have been among
the depression's causes. The "Live Poultry Code" as involved in the Schechter case regulated the marketing in
New York City of poultry much of which had been*

*brought from other states; it also fixed hours and wages
and working conditions of employees.*

*Although the several codes of fair competition were in
general authorized by the statute, they were worked out
by representatives of the industries affected and by government officials, and were subject to modification by the
executive. The codes were widely believed to be unconstitutional because of the largely unrestrained delegation
of legislative power, as discussed in* Panama Refining
Company v. Ryan, 293 U.S. 388 (1935). *They were believed vulnerable also in so far as they attempted to regulate commerce before interstate shipment had begun or
after it had ceased, as in the instance of the Schechter
case. The Supreme Court unanimously found the statute
unconstitutional on both grounds, thereby in effect de-
stroying the code structure. This decision, coupled with
others handed down in the same period, did much to
persuade President Roosevelt to make in 1937 his ill-
fated attempt to pack the Supreme Court with new members sympathetic with his program.*

✓   ✓   ✓

[Mr. Chief Justice Hughes] . . . . Two preliminary
points are stressed by the Government with respect to
the appropriate approach to the important questions
presented. We are told that the provision of the statute
authorizing the adoption of codes must be reviewed in
the light of the grave national crisis with which Congress
was confronted. Undoubtedly, the conditions to which
power is addressed are always to be considered when the
exercise of power is challenged. Extraordinary conditions
may call for extraordinary remedies. But the argument
necessarily stops short of an attempt to justify action
which lies outside the sphere of constitutional authority.
Extraordinary conditions do not create or enlarge constitutional power. The Constitution establishes a national
government with powers deemed to be adequate, as they
have proved to be both in war and peace, but these powers of the national government are limited by the constitutional grants. Those who act under these grants are
not at liberty to transcend the imposed limits because
they believe that more or different power is necessary.
Such assertions of extra-constitutional authority were

anticipated and precluded by the explicit terms of the Tenth Amendment,—"The powers not delegated to the United States by the Constitution, nor prohibited by it to the States, are reserved to the States respectively, or to the people."

The further point is urged that the national crisis demanded a broad and intensive cooperative effort by those engaged in trade and industry, and that this necessary cooperation was sought to be fostered by permitting them to initiate the adoption of codes. But the statutory plan is not simply one for voluntary effort. It does not seek merely to endow voluntary trade or industrial associations or groups with privileges or immunities. It involves the coercive exercise of the law-making power. The codes of fair competition which the statute attempts to authorize are codes of laws. If valid, they place all persons within their reach under the obligation of positive law, binding equally those who assent and those who do not assent. Violations of the provisions of the codes are punishable as crimes. . . .

We pointed out in the Panama Refining Company Case that the Constitution has never been regarded as denying to Congress the necessary resources of flexibility and practicality, which will enable it to perform its function in laying down policies and establishing standards, while leaving to selected instrumentalities the making of subordinate rules within prescribed limits and the determination of facts to which the policy as declared by the legislature is to apply. But we said that the constant recognition of the necessity and validity of such provisions, and the wide range of administrative authority which has been developed by means of them, cannot be allowed to obscure the limitations of the authority to delegate, if our constitutional system is to be maintained. . . .

The Act does not define "fair competition." "Unfair competition," as known to the common law, is a limited concept. Primarily, and strictly, it relates to the palming off of one's goods as those of a rival trader. . . . In recent years, its scope has been extended. It has been held to apply to misappropriation as well as misrepresentation, to the selling of another's goods as one's own —to misappropriation of what equitably belongs to a competitor. . . . Unfairness in competition has been predicated of acts which lie outside the ordinary course of business and are tainted by fraud, or coercion, or conduct otherwise prohibited by law. . . . But it is evident that in its widest range "unfair competition," as it has been understood in the law, does not reach the objectives of the codes which are authorized by the National Industrial Recovery Act. The codes may, indeed, cover conduct which existing law condemns, but they are not limited to conduct of that sort. The Government does not contend that the Act contemplates such a limitation. It would be opposed both to the declared purposes of the Act and to its administrative construction. . . .

The question, then, turns upon the authority which Section 3 of the Recovery Act vests in the President to approve or prescribe. If the codes have standing as penal statutes, this must be due to the effect of the executive action. But Congress cannot delegate legislative power to the President to exercise an unfettered discretion to make whatever laws he thinks may be needed or advisable for the rehabilitation and expansion of trade or industry. . . .

To summarize and conclude upon this point: Section 3 of the Recovery Act is without precedent. It supplies no standards for any trade, industry or activity. It does not undertake to prescribe rules of conduct to be applied to particular states of fact determined by appropriate administrative procedure. Instead of prescribing rules of conduct, it authorizes the making of codes to prescribe them. For that legislative undertaking, Section 3 sets up no standards, aside from the statement of the general aims of rehabilitation, correction and expansion described in Section 1. In view of the scope of that broad declaration, and of the nature of the few restrictions that are imposed, the discretion of the President in approving or prescribing codes, and thus enacting laws for the government of trade and industry throughout the country, is virtually unfettered. We think that the code-making authority thus conferred is an unconstitutional delegation of legislative power.

Third. The question of the application of the provisions of the Live Poultry Code to intrastate commerce. . . .

These provisions relate to the hours and wages of those employed by defendants in their slaughterhouse in Brooklyn and to the sales there made to retail dealers and butchers.

(1) Were these transactions *"in"* interstate commerce? Much is made of the fact that almost all the poultry coming to New York is sent there from other States. But the code provisions, as here applied, do not concern the transportation of the poultry from other States to New York, or the transactions of the commission men or others to whom it is consigned, or the sales made by such consignees to defendants. When defendants had made their purchases, whether at the West Washington Market in New York City or at the railroad terminals serving the City, or elsewhere, the poultry was trucked to their slaughterhouses in Brooklyn for local disposition. The interstate transaction in relation to that poultry then ended. Defendants held the poultry at their slaughterhouse markets for slaughter and local sale to retail dealers and butchers who in turn sold directly to consumers. Neither the slaughtering nor the sales by defendants were transactions in interstate commerce. . . .

The undisputed facts thus afford no warrant for the argument that the poultry handled by defendants at their slaughterhouse markets was in a *"current"* or *"flow"* of interstate commerce and was thus subject to congressional regulation. The mere fact that there may be a constant flow of commodities into a State does not mean that the flow continues after the property has arrived and has become commingled with the mass of property within the State and is there held solely for local disposition and use. So far as the poultry here in question is concerned, the flow in interstate commerce had ceased. The poultry had come to a permanent rest within the State. It was not held, used, or sold by defendants in relation to any further transactions in interstate commerce and was not destined for transportation to other States. Hence, decisions which deal with a stream of interstate commerce—where goods come to rest within a State temporarily and are later to go forward in interstate commerce—and with the regulations of transactions involved in that practical continuity of movement, are not applicable here. . . .

(2) Did the defendants' transactions directly *"affect"* interstate commerce so as to be subject to federal regulation? The power of Congress extends not only to the regulation of transactions which are part of interstate commerce, but to the protection of that commerce from injury. . . .

In determining how far the federal government may go in controlling intrastate transactions upon the ground that they "affect" interstate commerce, there is a necessary and well-established distinction between direct and indirect effects. The precise line can be drawn only as individual cases arise, but the distinction is clear in principle. Direct effects are illustrated by the railroad cases we have cited, as *e.g.,* the effect of failure to use prescribed safety appliances on railroads which are the highways of both interstate and intrastate commerce, injury to employees engaged in interstate transportation by the negligence of an employee engaged in an intrastate movement, the fixing of rates for intrastate transportation which unjustly discriminate against interstate commerce. But where the effect of intrastate transactions upon interstate commerce is merely indirect, such transactions remain within the domain of state power. If the commerce clause were construed to reach all enterprises and transactions which could be said to have an indirect effect upon interstate commerce, the federal authority would embrace practically all the activities of the people and the authority of the State over its domestic concerns would exist only by sufferance of the federal government. Indeed, on such a theory, even the development of the State's commercial facilities would be subject to federal control. . . .

We are of the opinion that the attempt through the provisions of the Code to fix the hours and wages of employees of defendants in their intrastate business was not a valid exercise of federal power. . . .

In view of these conclusions, we find it unnecessary to discuss other questions which have been raised as to the validity of certain provisions of the Code under the due process clause of the Fifth Amendment.

On both the grounds we have discussed, the attempted delegation of legislative power, and the attempted regulation of intrastate transactions which affect interstate commerce only indirectly, we hold the code provisions here in question to be invalid and that the judgment of conviction must be reversed.

— 28 —

NATIONAL LABOR RELATIONS BOARD v. JONES & LAUGHLIN STEEL CORPORATION

301 U.S. 1 (1937)

This case, decided by a vote of five to four, marked the beginnings of a new trend in determining the scope of the commerce power. The tone of the majority opinion is very different from that of opinions in 1935 and 1936 when the power was interpreted narrowly both as to regulation of activities before shipment began and activities which followed shipment across state lines. Pursuant to the National Labor Relations Act, the National Labor Relations Board had here attempted to regulate labor relations in a huge steel plant. The labor involved was not directly connected with actual shipment of goods. However, the Board provided two lines of argument to justify federal regulation. It contended that, on a parallel with the slaughtering and meat-packing business in Chicago, Stafford v. Wallace, 258 U.S. 495 (1922), the manufacture of steel in a Pennsylvania plant was but part of a stream of commerce which began with the shipment of iron ore from distant states and ended only with the delivery of the finished products; this entire stream was subject to federal regulation under the commerce clause. The Board contended also that, whether or not the processes of manufacture were themselves interstate commerce, labor disturbances in the plant would restrain interstate commerce and were there-

*fore subject to regulation as in the Shreveport Case, 234
U.S. 342 (1914). The Supreme Court adopted the latter
argument to uphold the exercise of federal power. To
people hitherto critical of the Supreme Court's handling
of the New Deal program, this decision suggested that
the Court might be expected to uphold New Deal legislation if Congress would but enact statutes that were
constitutional. Thus, in addition to paving the way for
broader federal regulation via the commerce power, the
decision probably played a part in defeating the attempt
to pack the Supreme Court with new appointees.*

✓　　　　　✓　　　　　✓

[Mr. Chief Justice Hughes] . . . . The facts as to the
nature and scope of the business of the Jones & Laughlin
Steel Corporation have been found by the Labor Board
and, so far as they are essential to the determination of
this controversy, they are not in dispute. The Labor
Board has found: The corporation is organized under
the laws of Pennsylvania and has its principal office at
Pittsburgh. It is engaged in the business of manufacturing iron and steel in plants situated in Pittsburgh and
nearby Aliquippa, Pennsylvania. It manufactures and
distributes a widely diversified line of steel and pig iron,
being the fourth largest producer of steel in the United
States. With its subsidiaries—nineteen in number—it is
a completely integrated enterprise, owning and operating
ore, coal and limestone properties, lake and river transportation facilities and terminal railroads located at its
manufacturing plants. It owns or controls mines in
Michigan and Minnesota. It operates four ore steamships
on the Great Lakes, used in the transportation of ore to
its factories. It owns coal mines in Pennsylvania. It operates towboats and steam barges used in carrying coal
to its factories. It owns limestone properties in various
places in Pennsylvania and West Virginia. It owns the
Monongahela connecting railroad which connects the
plants of the Pittsburgh works and forms an intercon-
nection with the Pennsylvania, New York Central and
Baltimore and Ohio Railroad systems. It owns the Aliquippa and Southern Railroad Company which connects
the Aliquippa works with the Pittsburgh and Lake Erie,

part of the New York Central system. Much of its product is shipped to its warehouses in Chicago, Detroit,
Cincinnati and Memphis,—to the last two places by
means of its own barges and transportation equipment.
In Long Island City, New York, and in New Orleans
it operates structural steel fabricating shops in connection with the warehousing of semi-finished materials
sent from its works. Through one of its wholly-owned
subsidiaries it owns, leases and operates stores, warehouses and yards for the distribution of equipment and
supplies for drilling and operating oil and gas mills and
for pipe lines, refineries and pumping stations. It has
sales offices in twenty cities in the United States and a
wholly-owned subsidiary which is devoted exclusively to
distributing its product in Canada. Approximately 75
per cent. of its product is shipped out of Pennsylvania.

Summarizing these operations, the Labor Board concluded that the works in Pittsburgh and Aliquippa "might
be likened to the heart of a self-contained, highly-
integrated body. They draw in the raw materials from
Michigan, Minnesota, West Virginia, Pennsylvania in
part through arteries and by means controlled by the
respondent; they transform the materials and then pump
them out to all parts of the nation through the vast
mechanism which the respondent has elaborated." . . .

First. The scope of the Act.—The Act is challenged
in its entirety as an attempt to regulate all industry,
thus invading the reserved powers of the States over their
local concerns. It is asserted that the references in the
Act to interstate and foreign commerce are colorable
at best; that the Act is not a true regulation of such
commerce or of matters which directly affect it but on
the contrary has the fundamental object of placing under
the compulsory supervision of the federal government
all industrial labor relations within the nation. . . .

We think it clear that the National Labor Relations
Act may be construed so as to operate within the sphere
of constitutional authority. . . . The grant of authority
to the Board does not purport to extend to the relationship between all industrial employers and employees. Its
terms do not impose collective bargaining upon all industry regardless of effects upon interstate or foreign
commerce. It purports to reach only what may be

deemed to burden or obstruct that commerce and, thus qualified, it must be construed as contemplating the exercise of control within constitutional bounds. It is a familiar principle that acts which directly burden or obstruct interstate or foreign commerce, or its free flow, are within the reach of congressional power. Acts having that effect are not rendered immune because they grow out of labor disputes. . . . It is the effect upon commerce, not the source of the injury, which is the criterion. . . . Whether or not particular action does affect commerce in such a close and intimate fashion as to be subject to federal control, and hence to lie within the authority conferred upon the Board, is left by the statute to be determined as individual cases arise. We are thus to inquire whether in the instant case the constitutional boundary has been passed.

Second. The unfair labor practices in question. . . .

Thus, in its present application, the statute goes no further than to safeguard the right of employees to self-organization and to select representatives of their own choosing for collective bargaining or other mutual protection without restraint or coercion by their employer.

That is a fundamental right. Employees have as clear a right to organize and select their representatives for lawful purposes as the respondent has to organize its business and select its own officers and agents. Discrimination and coercion to prevent the free exercise of the right of employees to self-organization and representation is a proper subject for condemnation by competent legislative authority. Long ago we stated the reason for labor organizations. We said that they were organized out of the necessities of the situation; that a single employee was helpless in dealing with an employer; that he was dependent ordinarily on his daily wage for the maintenance of himself and family; that if the employer refused to pay him the wages that he thought fair, he was nevertheless unable to leave the employ and resist arbitrary and unfair treatment; that union was essential to give laborers opportunity to deal on an equality with their employers. . . .

We do not find it necessary to determine whether these features of defendant's business dispose of the asserted analogy to the "stream of commerce" cases. The instances in which that metaphor has been used are but particular, and not exclusive, illustrations of the protective power which the Government invokes in support of the present Act. The congressional authority to protect interstate commerce from burdens and obstructions is not limited to transactions which can be deemed to be an essential part of a "flow" of interstate or foreign commerce. Burdens and obstructions may be due to injurious action springing from other sources. The fundamental principle is that the power to regulate commerce is the power to enact "all appropriate legislation" for "its protection and advancement" . . . ; to adopt measures "to promote its growth and insure its safety" . . . ; "to foster, protect, control and restrain." . . . That power is plenary and may be exerted to protect interstate commerce "no matter what the source of the dangers which threaten it." . . . Although activities may be intrastate in character when separately considered, if they have such a close and substantial relation to interstate commerce that their control is essential or appropriate to protect that commerce from burdens and obstructions, Congress cannot be denied the power to exercise that control. . . . Undoubtedly the scope of this power must be considered in the light of our dual system of government and may not be extended so as to embrace effects upon interstate commerce so indirect and remote that to embrace them, in view of our complex society, would effectually obliterate the distinction between what is national and what is local and create a completely centralized government. . . . The question is necessarily one of degree. . . .

It is thus apparent that the fact that the employees here concerned were engaged in production is not determinative. The question remains as to the effect upon interstate commerce of the labor practice involved. In [the Schechter case], we found that the effect there was so remote as to be beyond the federal power. To find "immediacy or directness" there was to find it "almost everywhere," a result inconsistent with the maintenance of our federal system. In the Carter case [298 U.S. 238 (1936)], the Court was of the opinion that the provisions of the statute relating to production were invalid upon several grounds,—that there was improper delegation of legislative power, and that the requirements not only went beyond any sustainable measure of protection of interstate commerce but were also inconsistent with due process. These cases are not controlling here.

Fourth. Effects of the unfair labor practice in respondent's enterprise.—Giving full weight to respondent's contention with respect to a break in the complete continuity of the "stream of commerce" by reason of respondent's manufacturing operations, the fact remains that the stoppage of those operations by industrial strife would have a most serious effect upon interstate commerce. In view of the respondent's far-flung activities, it is idle to say that the effect would be indirect or remote. It is obvious that it would be immediate and might be catastrophic. We are asked to shut our eyes to the plainest facts of our national life and to deal with the question of direct and indirect effects in an intellectual vacuum. Because there may be but indirect and remote effects upon interstate commerce in connection with a host of local enterprises throughout the country, it does not follow that other industrial activities do not have such a close and intimate relation to interstate commerce as to make the presence of industrial strife a matter of the most urgent national concern. When industries organize themselves on a national scale, making their relation to interstate commerce the dominant factor in their activities, how can it be maintained that their industrial labor relations constitute a forbidden field into which Congress may not enter when it is necessary to protect interstate commerce from the paralyzing consequences of industrial war? We have often said that interstate commerce itself is a practical conception. It is equally true that interferences with that commerce must be appraised by a judgment that does not ignore actual experience.

Experience has abundantly demonstrated that the recognition of the right of employees to self-organization and to have representatives of their own choosing for the purpose of collective bargaining is often an essential condition of industrial peace. Refusal to confer and negotiate has been one of the most prolific causes of strife. This is such an outstanding fact in the history of labor disturbances that it is a proper subject of judicial notice and requires no citation of instances. . . .

These questions have frequently engaged the attention of Congress and have been the subject of many inquiries. The steel industry is one of the great basic industries of the United States, with ramifying activities affecting interstate commerce at every point. The Government aptly refers to the steel strike of 1919-1920 with its far-reaching consequences. The fact that there appears to have been no major disturbance in that industry in the more recent period did not dispose of the possibilities of future and like dangers to interstate commerce which Congress was entitled to foresee and to exercise its protective power to forestall. It is not necessary again to detail the facts as to respondent's enterprise. Instead of being beyond the pale, we think that it presents in a most striking way the close and intimate relation which a manufacturing industry may have to interstate commerce and we have no doubt that Congress had constitutional authority to safeguard the right of respondent's employees to self-organization and freedom in the choice of representatives for collective bargaining.

— 29 —

CHAMBERS v. FLORIDA

309 U.S. 227 (1940)

Fairness of treatment to oppressed peoples and even to those accused of crime has been one of the cardinal principles not only specifically of due process of law but of our constitutional system as a whole. There have been times when the ideal was far from realized where our Negro population was concerned, and particularly with respect to those Negroes accused of crime. When after the appointment of Justice Black to the Supreme Court in 1937 it was discovered that he had once been

*a member of the Ku Klux Klan, it was feared that the
new justice from Alabama might appear at least as a
laggard in defense of the rights of colored people. Early
in 1940, the Supreme Court heard argument in a case
from Florida in which a group of Negroes had been
convicted of robbery and murder on the basis of confessions extorted by the overwhelming pressures of police
questioning. The case was decided on February 12th that
year, the birthday of Abraham Lincoln, author of the
Proclamation of Emancipation, and Justice Black wrote
the opinion for a unanimous Supreme Court, asserting
the right of the defendants to the protection of the Fourteenth Amendment against conviction on the basis of
extorted confessions.*

✦   ✦   ✦

[Mr. Justice Black] . . . . The scope and operation
of the Fourteenth Amendment have been fruitful sources
of controversy in our constitutional history. However, in
view of its historical setting and the wrongs which called
it into being, the due process provision of the Fourteenth
Amendment—just as that in the Fifth—has led few to
doubt that it was intended to guarantee procedural
standards adequate and appropriate, then and thereafter,
to protect, at all times, people charged with or suspected
of crime by those holding positions of power and authority. Tyrannical governments had immemorially uti-
lized dictatorial criminal procedures and punishment to
make scape goats of the weak, or of helpless political,
religious, or racial minorities and those who differed,
who would not conform and who resisted tyranny. The
instruments of such governments were in the main, two.
Conduct, innocent when engaged in, was subsequently
made by fiat criminally punishable without legislation.
And a liberty loving people won the principle that criminal punishments could not be inflicted save for that
which proper legislative action had already by "the law
of the land" forbidden when done. But even more was
needed. From the popular hatred and abhorrence of
illegal confinement, torture and extortion of confessions
of violations of the "law of the land" evolved the fundamental idea that no man's life, liberty or property be
forfeited as criminal punishment for violation of that

law until there had been a charge fairly made and fairly
tried in a public tribunal free of prejudice, passion, excitement and tyrannical power. Thus, as assurance against
ancient evils, our country, in order to preserve "the
blessings of liberty," wrote into its basic law the requirement, among others, that the forfeiture of the lives,
liberties or property of people accused of crime can only
follow if procedural safeguards of due process have been
obeyed.

The determination to preserve an accused's right to
procedural due process sprang in large part from knowledge of the historical truth that the rights and liberties
of people accused of crime could not be safely entrusted
to secret inquisitorial processes. The testimony of cen-
turies, in governments of varying kinds over populations
of different races and beliefs, stood as proof that psysical
and mental torture and coercion had brought about the
tragically unjust sacrifices of some who were the noblest
and most useful of their generations. The rack, the
thumbscrew, the wheel, solitary confinement, protracted
questioning and cross questioning, and other ingenious
forms of entrapment of the helpless or unpopular had
left their wake of mutilated bodies and shattered minds
along the way to the cross, the guillotine, the stake and
the hangman's noose. And they who have suffered most
from secret and dictatorial proceedings have almost always been the poor, the ignorant, the numerically weak,
the friendless, and the powerless.

This requirement—of conforming to fundamental
standards of procedure in criminal trials—was made operative against the States by the Fourteenth Amendment.
Where one of several accused had limped into the trial
court as a result of admitted physical mistreatment inflicted to obtain confessions upon which a jury had
returned a verdict of guilty of murder, this Court recently declared, Brown v. Mississippi, . . . that "It
would be difficult to conceive of methods more revolting
to the sense of justice than those taken to procure the
confessions of these petitioners, and the use of the confessions thus obtained as the basis for conviction and
sentence was a clear denial of due process."

Here, the record develops a sharp conflict upon the
issue of physical violence and mistreatment, but shows,

without conflict, the drag net methods of arrest on sus-
picion without warrant, and the protracted questioning
and cross questioning of these ignorant young colored
tenant farmers by State officers and other white citizens,
in a fourth floor jail room, where as prisoners they were
without friends, advisers or counselors, and under circumstances calculated to break the strongest nerves and
the stoutest resistance. Just as our decision in Brown v.
Mississippi was based upon the fact that the confessions
were the result of compulsion, so in the present case, the
admitted practices were such as to justify the statement
that "The undisputed facts showed that compulsion was
applied."

For five days petitioners were subjected to interrogations culminating in Saturday's (May 20th) all night
examination. Over a period of five days they steadily
refused to confess and disclaimed any guilt. The very
circumstances surrounding their confinement and their
questioning without any formal charges having been
brought, were such as to fill petitioners with terror and
frightful misgivings. Some were practical strangers in
the community; three were arrested in a one-room farm
tenant house which was their home; the haunting fear of
mob violence was around them in an atmosphere charged
with excitement and public indignation. From virtually
the moment of their arrest until their eventual confessions, they never knew just when anyone would be
called back to the fourth floor room, and there, sur-
rounded by his accusers and others, interrogated by men
who held their very lives—so far as these ignorant petitioners could know—in the balance. The rejection of
petitioner Woodward's first "confession," given in the
early hours of Sunday morning, because it was found
wanting, demonstrates the relentless tenacity which
"broke" petitioners' will and rendered them helpless to
resist their accusers further. To permit human lives to
be forfeited upon confessions thus obtained would make
of the constitutional requirement of due process of law
a meaningless symbol.

We are not impressed by the argument that law enforcement methods such as those under review are necessary to uphold our laws. The Constitution proscribes
such lawless means irrespective of the end. And this

argument flouts the basic principle that all people must stand on an equality before the bar of justice in every American court. Today, as in ages past, we are not without tragic proof that the exalted power of some governments to punish manufactured crime dictatorially is the handmaid of tyranny. Under our constitutional system, courts stand against any winds that blow as havens of refuge for those who might otherwise suffer because they are helpless, weak, outnumbered, or because they are non-conforming victims of prejudice and public excitement. Due process of law, preserved for all by our Constitution, commands that no such practice as that disclosed by this record shall send any accused to his death. No higher duty, no more solemn responsibility, rests upon this Court, than that of translating into living law and maintaining this constitutional shield deliberately planned and inscribed for the benefit of every human being subject to our Constitution—of whatever race, creed or persuasion.

— 30 —

KOREMATSU v. UNITED STATES

323 U.S. 214 (1944)

The Japanese attack on Pearl Harbor on December 7, 1941, which destroyed or immobilized much of our Pacific fleet, provoked fear of attack on the West Coast of the United States which might be aided by Japanese agents among the large numbers of American citizens of Japanese ancestry. It was assumed that there was inadequate time for screening members of the race in question for such disloyal persons and that in the emergency it was necessary immediately to isolate all persons of Japanese ancestry from military installations and remove them from critical areas. A combination of an act of

Congress and an Executive Order of the President and orders of the military commander on the Pacific Coast brought first a curfew program for Japanese-Americans and then their removal from critical areas and, then for some of them, incarceration in what were called relocation centers—all without any findings of fact as to misbehavior of any kind and in spite of the fact that most of the persons involved were American citizens. People not too concerned with national survival to consider matters of constitutional right were deeply troubled by this invasion of the lives of people who were not even accused of misbehavior, especially since the invasion took place along racial lines. The Supreme Court in 1943, nevertheless, held that the curfew order had been a proper exercise of the war power. In 1944, when the West Coast crisis was definitely past, it held that the detention in relocation centers had been illegal, not on constitutional grounds but on the ground that the executive order and the statute when properly interpreted did not authorize such detention. In the Korematsu case, however, which is here presented in part, the Court, by a vote of six to three, upheld the removal of persons of Japanese extraction from critical areas. The majority opinion by Justice Black attempted to portray the lawfulness of the action, whereas the excerpts from the dissent by Justice Jackson indicate the problems involved in judicial appraisal of the lawfulness of military orders issued in time of crisis.

✓   ✓   ✓

[Mr. Justice Black] . . . . Like curfew, exclusion of those of Japanese origin was deemed necessary because of the presence of an unascertained number of disloyal members of the group, most of whom we have no doubt were loyal to this country. It was because we could not reject the finding of the military authorities that it was impossible to bring about an immediate segregation of the disloyal from the loyal that we sustained the validity of the curfew order as applying to the whole group. In the instant case, temporary exclusion of the entire group was rested by the military on the same ground. The judgment that exclusion of the whole group was for the same reason a military imperative answers the contention that the exclusion was in the nature of group punishment based on antagonism to those of Japanese origin. That there were members of the group who retained loyalties to Japan has been confirmed by investigations made subsequent to the exclusion. Approximately five thousand American citizens of Japanese ancestry refused to swear unqualified allegiance to the United States and to renounce allegiance to the Japanese Emperor, and several thousand evacuees requested repatriation to Japan.

We uphold the exclusion order as of the time it was made and when the petitioner violated it. . . . In doing so, we are not unmindful of the hardships imposed by it upon a large group of American citizens. . . . But hardships are part of war, and war is an aggregation of hardships. All citizens alike, both in and out of uniform, feel the impact of war in greater or lesser measure. Citizenship has its responsibilities as well as its privileges, and in time of war the burden is always heavier. Compulsory exclusion of large groups of citizens from their homes, except under circumstances of direct emergency and peril, is inconsistent with our basic governmental institutions. But when under conditions of modern warfare our shores are threatened by hostile forces, the power to protect must be commensurate with the threatened danger. . . .

It is said that we are dealing here with the case of imprisonment of a citizen in a concentration camp solely because of his ancestry, without evidence or inquiry concerning his loyalty and good disposition towards the United States. Our task would be simple, our duty clear, were this a case involving the imprisonment of a loyal citizen in a concentration camp because of racial prejudice. Regardless of the true nature of the assembly and relocation centers—and we deem it unjustifiable to call them concentration camps with all the ugly connotations that term implies—we are dealing specifically with nothing but an exclusion order. To cast this case into outlines of racial prejudice, without reference to the real military dangers which were presented, merely confuses the issue. Korematsu was not excluded from the Military Area because of hostility to him or his race. He *was* excluded because we are at war with the Japanese Empire, because the properly constituted military authorities feared an invasion of our West Coast and felt constrained to take proper security measures, because they decided that the military urgency of the situation demanded that all citizens of Japanese ancestry be segregated from the West Coast temporarily, and finally, because Congress, reposing its confidence in this time of war in our military leaders—as inevitably it must—determined that they should have the power to do just this. There was evidence of disloyalty on the part of some, the military authorities considered that the need for action was great, and time was short. We cannot—by availing ourselves of the calm perspective of hindsight—now say that at that time these actions were unjustified. . . .

[Mr. Justice Jackson, dissenting] . . . . But the "law" which this prisoner is convicted of disregarding is not found in an act of Congress, but in a military order. Neither the Act of Congress nor the Executive Order of the President, nor both together, would afford a basis for this conviction. It rests on the orders of General DeWitt. And it is said that if the military commander had reasonable military grounds for promulgating the orders, they are constitutional and become law, and the Court is required to enforce them. There are several reasons why I cannot subscribe to this doctrine.

It would be impracticable and dangerous idealism to expect or insist that each specific military command in an area of probable operations will conform to conventional tests of constitutionality. When an area is so beset that it must be put under military control at all, the paramount consideration is that its measures be successful, rather than legal. The armed services must protect a society, not merely its Constitution. The very essence of the military job is to marshal physical force, to remove every obstacle to its effectiveness, to give it every strategic advantage. Defense measures will not, and often should not, be held within the limits that bind civil authority in peace. No court can require such a commander in such circumstances to act as a reasonable man; he may be unreasonably cautious and exacting. Perhaps he should be. But a commander in temporarily focusing the life of a community on defense is carrying out a military program; he is not making law in the sense the courts know the term. He issues orders, and they may have a certain authority as military commands, although they may be very bad as constitutional law.

But if we cannot confine military expedients by the Constitution, neither would I distort the Constitution to approve all that the military may deem expedient. That is what the Court appears to be doing, whether consciously or not. I cannot say, from any evidence before me, that the orders of General DeWitt were not reasonably expedient military precautions, nor could I say that they were. But even if they were permissible military procedures, I deny that it follows that they are constitutional. If, as the Court holds, it does follow, then we may as well say that any military order will be constitutional and have done with it. . . .

Much is said of the danger to liberty from the Army program for deporting and detaining these citizens of Japanese extraction. But a judicial construction of the due process clause that will sustain this order is a far more subtle blow to liberty than the promulgation of the order itself. A military order, however unconstitutional, is not apt to last longer than the military emergency. Even during that period a succeeding commander may revoke it all. But once a judicial opinion rationalizes such an order to show that it conforms to the Constitution, or rather rationalizes the Constitution to show that the Constitution sanctions such an order, the Court for all time has validated the principle of racial discrimination in criminal procedure and of transplanting American citizens. The principle then lies about like a loaded weapon ready for the hand of any authority that can bring forward a plausible claim of an urgent need. Every repetition imbeds that principle more deeply in our law and thinking and expands it to new purposes. All who observe the work of courts are familiar with what Judge Cardozo described as "the tendency of a principle to expand itself to the limit of its logic." A military commander may overstep the bounds of constitutionality, and it is an incident. But if we review and approve, that passing incident becomes the doctrine of the Constitution. There it has a generative power of its own, and all that it creates will be in its own image. Nothing better illustrates this danger than does the Court's opinion in this case. . . .

YOUNGSTOWN SHEET & TUBE COMPANY v. SAWYER

343 U.S. 579 (1952)

Throughout the New Deal period and the period of World War II, the presidency won increasing power within the federal government, both as a result of grants of power by Congress and through the interpretation of the powers of the presidential office. It was perhaps inevitable that this expansion should at some time be checked. The check came in the Youngstown decision during the period of the Korean crisis in the early 1950's. Failing to get a satisfactory bargaining agreement with the steel industry, the union gave notice of a strike, one which might imperil the equipment of our forces in Korea. The President was unable to avert the strike through the use of such federal agencies as were available. Deeming too cumbersome and time-consuming the procedures of the Selective Service Act and the Defense Production Act, pursuant to which property might be seized under certain circumstances, President Truman directed the Secretary of Commerce, Charles Sawyer, to take over and operate the industry so that production might continue without interruption. By a vote of six to three the Supreme Court held that the President had no constitutional power to take over the industry without authorization by statute. So diverse were the patterns of individual reasoning among the majority justices that each of the five who concurred in the majority opinion of Justice Black wrote also a separate opinion of his own. Because of the diversity, the only thing we can assert with confidence is that in some degree the enhancement of the power of the presidential office has been restrained.

↗   ↗   ↗

[Mr. Justice Black] . . . . We are asked to decide whether the President was acting within his constitutional power when he issued an order directing the Secretary of Commerce to take possession of and operate most of the Nation's steel mills. The mill owners argue that the President's order amounts to lawmaking, a legislative function which the Constitution has expressly confided to the Congress and not to the President. The Government's position is that the order was made on findings of the President that his action was necessary to avert a national catastrophe which would inevitably result from a stoppage of steel production, and that in meeting this grave emergency the President was acting within the aggregate of his constitutional powers as the Nation's Chief Executive and the Commander in Chief of the Armed Forces of the United States. . . .

The President's power, if any, to issue the order must stem either from an act of Congress or from the Constitution itself. There is no statute that expressly authorizes the President to take possession of property as he did here. Nor is there any act of Congress to which our attention has been directed from which such a power can fairly be implied. Indeed, we do not understand the Government to rely on statutory authorization for this seizure. There are two statutes which do authorize the President to take both personal and real property under certain conditions. However, the Government admits that these conditions were not met and that the President's order was not rooted in either of the statutes. The Government refers to the seizure provisions of one of these statutes (section 201 (b) of the Defense Production Act) as "much too cumbersome, involved, and time-consuming for the crisis which was at hand."

Moreover, the use of the seizure technique to solve labor disputes in order to prevent work stoppages was not only unauthorized by any congressional enactment; prior to this controversy, Congress had refused to adopt that method of settling labor disputes. When the Taft-Hartley Act was under consideration in 1947, Congress rejected an amendment which would have authorized such governmental seizures in cases of emergency. Apparently it was thought that the technique of seizure, like that of compulsory arbitration, would interfere with the process of collective bargaining. Consequently, the plan Congress adopted in that Act did not provide for seizure under any circumstances. Instead, the plan sought to bring about settlements by use of the customary devices of mediation, conciliation, investigation by boards of inquiry, and public reports. In some instances temporary injunctions were authorized to provide cooling-off periods. All this failing, unions were left free to strike after a secret vote by employees as to whether they wished to accept their employer's final settlement offer.

It is clear that if the President had authority to issue the order he did, it must be found in some provision of the Constitution. And it is not claimed that express constitutional language grants this power to the President. The contention is that presidential power should be implied from the aggregate of his powers under the Constitution. Particular reliance is placed on provisions in Article II which say that "The executive Power shall be vested in a President . . ."; that "he shall take Care that the Laws be faithfully executed"; and that he "shall be Commander in Chief of the Army and Navy of the United States."

The order cannot properly be sustained as an exercise of the President's military power as Commander in Chief of the Armed Forces. The Government attempts to do so by citing a number of cases upholding broad powers in military commanders engaged in day-to-day fighting in a theater of war. Such cases need not concern us here. Even though "theater of war" be an expanding concept, we cannot with faithfulness to our constitutional system hold that the Commander in Chief of the Armed Forces has the ultimate power as such to take possession of private property in order to keep labor disputes from stopping production. This is a job for the Nation's lawmakers, not for its military authorities.

Nor can the seizure order be sustained because of the several constitutional provisions that grant executive power to the President. In the framework of our Constitution, the President's power to see that the laws are faithfully executed refutes the idea that he is to be a lawmaker. The Constitution limits his functions in the lawmaking process to the recommending of laws he thinks wise and the vetoing of laws he thinks bad. And the Constitution is neither silent nor equivocal about who shall make laws which the President is to execute. The first section of the first article says that "All legislative Powers herein granted shall be vested in a Congress of the United States. . . ." After granting many powers to the Congress, Article I goes on to provide that Congress may "make all Laws which shall be necessary and proper for carrying into Execution the foregoing Powers, and all other Powers vested by this Constitution in the Government of the United States, or in any Department or Officer thereof."

The President's order does not direct that a congressional policy be executed in a manner prescribed by Congress—it directs that a presidential policy be executed in a manner prescribed by the President. The preamble of the order itself, like that of many statutes, sets out reasons why the President believes certain policies should be adopted, proclaims these policies as rules of conduct to be followed, and again, like a statute, authorizes a government official to promulgate additional rules and regulations consistent with the policy proclaimed and needed to carry that policy into execution. The power of Congress to adopt such public policies as those proclaimed by the order is beyond question. It can authorize the taking of private property for public use. It can make laws regulating the relationships between employers and employees, prescribing rules designed to settle labor disputes, and fixing wages and working conditions in certain fields of our economy. The Constitution does not subject this lawmaking power of Congress to presidential or military supervision or control.

It is said that other Presidents without congressional authority have taken possession of private business enterprises in order to settle labor disputes. But even if this be true, Congress has not thereby lost its exclusive constitutional authority to make laws necessary and proper to carry out the powers vested by the Constitution "in the Government of the United States, or any Department or Officer thereof."

The Founders of this Nation entrusted the lawmaking power to the Congress alone in both good and bad times. It would do no good to recall the historical events, the fears of power and the hopes for freedom that lay behind their choice. Such a review would but confirm our holding that this seizure order cannot stand.

— 32 —

BROWN v. BOARD OF EDUCATION OF TOPEKA

347 U.S. 483 (1954)

Negro people in the United States and their white friends never willingly accepted the "separate but equal" doctrine of Plessy v. Ferguson (see Document No. 18). *For a long time it remained true as to transportation, education, recreation, and other fields that the equality which was provided was only nominal and not real, so that the battle for real equality had to go on even as it was contended that separation was itself inherently unequal. From the 1930's until the 1950's, the Supreme Court struck down provisions of various states for the higher or professional education of Negroes as failing to meet the requirements of equality. Particularly important were* McLaurin v. Oklahoma State Regents, *339 U.S. 637 (1950) and* Sweatt v. Painter, *339 U.S. 629 (1950). In the latter case counsel for the Negro involved challenged the separate but equal doctrine as well as the allegation of equality of facilities. Finding the facilities themselves unequal, the Supreme Court expressly left open the question of the continuing validity of the doctrine, thereby in effect inviting a direct challenge to the doctrine in other cases.*

The challenge came with the group of cases which are headed by the Brown case, wherein elementary educa-

tion rather than higher education was involved. The group of cases was argued twice, at great length, before the Court reached a decision. The decision was unanimous and the Court, contrary to recent practice except in the field of the delicate issues of racial discrimination, spoke through a single opinion with no overflow of concurring sentiments.

The cases were then argued again on the question of the method of enforcement. The Court then decided (349 U.S. 294) that the cases should be remanded to the lower courts, which were directed to "enter such orders and decrees consistent with this opinion as are necessary and proper to admit to public schools on a racially nondiscriminatory basis with all deliberate speed the parties to these cases."

✓   ✓   ✓

[Mr. Chief Justice Warren] . . . . These cases come to us from the States of Kansas, South Carolina, Virginia, and Delaware. They are premised on different facts and different local conditions, but a common legal question justifies their consideration together in this consolidated opinion.

In each of the cases, minors of the Negro race, through their legal representatives, seek the aid of the courts in obtaining admission to the public schools of their community on a nonsegregated basis. In each instance, they had been denied admission to schools attended by white children under laws requiring or permitting segregation according to race. This segregation was alleged to deprive the plaintiffs of the equal protection of the laws under the Fourteenth Amendment. In each of the cases other than the Delaware case, a three-judge federal district court denied relief to the plaintiffs on the so-called "separate but equal" doctrine announced by this Court in Plessy v. Ferguson, 163 U.S. 537. . . . Under that doctrine, equality of treatment is accorded when the races are provided substantially equal facilities, even though these facilities be separate. In the Delaware case, the Supreme Court of Delaware adhered to that doctrine, but ordered that the plaintiffs be admitted to the white schools because of their superiority to the Negro schools.

The plaintiffs contend that segregated public schools are not "equal" and cannot be made "equal," and that hence they are deprived of the equal protection of the laws. Because of the obvious importance of the question presented, the Court took jurisdiction. Argument was heard in the 1952 Term, and reargument was heard this Term on certain questions propounded by the Court.

Reargument was largely devoted to the circumstances surrounding the adoption of the Fourteenth Amendment in 1868. It covered exhaustively consideration of the Amendment in Congress, ratification by the states, then existing practices in racial segregation, and the views of proponents and opponents of the Amendment. This discussion and our own investigation convince us that, although these sources cast some light, it is not enough to resolve the problem with which we are faced. At best, they are inconclusive. The most avid proponents of the post-War Amendments undoubtedly intended them to remove all legal distinctions among "all persons born or naturalized in the United States." Their opponents, just as certainly, were antagonistic to both the letter and the spirit of the Amendments and wished them to have the most limited effect. What others in Congress and the state legislatures had in mind cannot be determined with any degree of certainty.

An additional reason for the inconclusive nature of the Amendment's history, with respect to segregated schools, is the status of public education at that time. In the South, the movement toward free common schools, supported by general taxation, had not yet taken hold. Education of white children was largely in the hands of private groups. Education of Negroes was almost nonexistent, and practically all of the race was illiterate. In fact, any education of Negroes was forbidden by law in some states. Today, in contrast, many Negroes have achieved outstanding success in the arts and sciences as well as in the business and professional world. It is true that public school education at the time of the Amendment had advanced further in the North, but the effect of the Amendment on Northern States was generally ignored in the congressional debates. Even in the North, the conditions of public education did not approximate those existing today. The curriculum was usually rudimentary; ungraded schools were common in rural areas; the school term was but three months a year in many states; and compulsory school attendance was virtually unknown. As a consequence, it is not surprising that there should be so little in the history of the Fourteenth Amendment relating to its intended effect on public education.

In the first cases in this Court construing the Fourteenth Amendment, decided shortly after its adoption, the Court interpreted it as proscribing all state-imposed discriminations against the Negro race. The doctrine of "separate but equal" did not make its appearance in this Court until 1896 in the case of Plessy v. Ferguson (US) supra, involving not education but transportation. American courts have since labored with the doctrine for over half a century. In this Court, there have been six cases involving the "separate but equal" doctrine in the field of public education. . . .

Here . . . there are findings below that the Negro and white schools involved have been equalized, or are being equalized, with respect to buildings, curricula, qualifications and salaries of teachers, and other "tangible" factors. Our decision, therefore, cannot turn on merely a comparison of these tangible factors in the Negro and white schools involved in each of the cases. We must look instead to the effect of segregation itself on public education.

In approaching this problem, we cannot turn the clock back to 1868 when the Amendment was adopted, or even to 1896 when Plessy v. Ferguson was written. We must consider public education in the light of its full development and its present place in American life throughout the Nation. Only in this way can it be determined if segregation in public schools deprives these plaintiffs of the equal protection of the laws.

Today, education is perhaps the most important function of state and local governments. Compulsory school attendance laws and the great expenditures for education both demonstrate our recognition of the importance of education to our democratic society. It is required in the performance of our most basic public responsibilities, even service in the armed forces. It is the very foundation of good citizenship. Today it is a principal instrument in awakening the child to cultural values, in preparing him for later professional training, and in helping him to adjust normally to his environment. In these days, it is doubtful that any child may reasonably be expected to succeed in life if he is denied the opportunity of an education. Such an opportunity, where the state has undertaken to provide it, is a right which must be made available to all on equal terms.

We come then to the question presented: Does segregation of children in public schools solely on the basis of race, even though the physical facilities and other "tangible" factors may be equal, deprive the children of the minority group of equal educational opportunities? We believe that it does.

In Sweatt v. Painter . . . in finding that a segregated law school for Negroes could not provide them equal educational opportunities, this Court relied in large part on "those qualities which are incapable of objective measurement but which make for greatness in a law school." In McLaurin v. Oklahoma State Regents, 339 US 637 . . . the Court, in requiring that a Negro admitted to a white graduate school be treated like all other students, again resorted to intangible considerations: ". . . his ability to study, to engage in discussions and exchange views with other students, and, in general, to learn his profession." Such considerations apply with added force to children in grade and high schools. To separate them from others of similar age and qualifications solely because of their race generates a feeling of inferiority as to their status in the community that may affect their hearts and minds in a way unlikely ever to be undone. The effect of this separation on their educational opportunities was well stated by a finding in the Kansas case by a court which nevertheless felt compelled to rule against the Negro plaintiffs:

"Segregation of white and colored children in public schools has a detrimental effect upon the colored children. The impact is greater when it has the sanction of the law; for the policy of separating the races is usually interpreted as denoting the inferiority of the negro group. A sense of inferiority affects the motivation of a child to learn. Segregation with the sanction of law, therefore, has a tendency to [retard] the educational and mental development of Negro children and to deprive them of some of the benefits they would receive in a racial[ly] integrated school system."

Whatever may have been the extent of psychological knowledge at the time of Plessy v. Ferguson, this finding is amply supported by modern authority. Any language in Plessy v. Ferguson contrary to this finding is rejected.

We conclude that in the field of public education the doctrine of "separate but equal" has no place. Separate educational facilities are inherently unequal. Therefore, we hold that the plaintiffs and others similarly situated for whom the actions have been brought are, by reason of the segregation complained of, deprived of the equal protection of the laws guaranteed by the Fourteenth Amendment. This disposition makes unnecessary any discussion whether such segregation also violates the Due Process Clause of the Fourteenth Amendment.

Because these are class actions, because of the wide applicability of this decision, and because of the great variety of local conditions, the formulation of decrees in these cases presents problems of considerable complexity. On reargument, the consideration of appropriate relief was necessarily subordinated to the primary question—the constitutionality of segregation in public education. We have now announced that such segregation is a denial of the equal protection of the laws.

— 33 —

WATKINS v. UNITED STATES

354 U.S. 178 (1957)

Article I of the Constitution states that "All legislative powers herein granted shall be vested in a Congress of the United States." The scope of federal legislative power is very broad—almost as broad as the scope of the Constitution itself. From the power to legislate is inferred the power to collect information to determine what legislation is or is not needed. With the growth in the complexity of our society it has been necessary to expand the investigative activities of Congress in order to measure the wisdom of proposed legislation. Recognizing the need for largely unhampered inquiry, federal courts have been hesitant to curb congressional investigatory power even when witnesses contended that inquiries invaded their constitutional right to privacy.

Yet investigations in the United States have long been regarded as having value beyond preparation for legislation. They have themselves been instruments of control —as witness the early state public utility commissions which were expected to alleviate evils by "pitiless publicity." The investigations of many congressional committees have been regarded as themselves instruments of purification, whether for the control of vice or communist affiliation or other disreputable activities. Reputations have been destroyed, positions have been lost and business losses have been incurred along a wide front merely as a result of investigative exposure and without resort to trial for violation of any law. In recent years there has been a growing body of sentiment, even within Congress itself, for curbing what in effect if not in law is direct punishment by investigating committees without the protections of judicial trial.

The Watkins case involved punishment of contempt for refusal to answer questions asked by the Committee on Un-American Activities of the House of Representatives. Watkins testified as to his own former collaboration with the Communist party but refused to disclose the names of other persons involved, saying that he did not believe that any law of the United States compelled him to make such disclosure. With only one justice dissenting, the Supreme Court here took an important step in narrowing the range of investigatory activity as used for the purpose of direct punishment, saying that "there is no congressional power to expose for the sake of exposure."

[Mr. Chief Justice Warren] . . . . We start with several basic premises on which there is general agreement. The power of the Congress to conduct investigations is inherent in the legislative process. That power is broad. It encompasses inquiries concerning the administration of existing laws as well as proposed or possibly needed statutes. It includes surveys of defects in our social, economic or political system for the purpose of enabling Congress to remedy them. It comprehends probes into departments of the Federal Government to expose corruption, inefficiency or waste. But broad as is this power of inquiry, it is not unlimited. There is no general authority to expose the private affairs of individuals without justification in terms of the functions of the Congress. This was freely conceded by the Solicitor General in his argument of this case. Nor is the Congress a law enforcement or trial agency. These are functions of the executive and judicial departments of government. No inquiry is an end in itself; it must be related to and in furtherance of a legitimate task of the Congress. Investigations conducted solely for the personal aggrandizement of the investigators or to "punish" those investigated are indefensible.

It is unquestionably the duty of all citizens to cooperate with the Congress in its efforts to obtain the facts needed for intelligent legislative action. It is their unremitting obligation to respond to subpoenas, to respect the dignity of the Congress and its committees and to testify fully with respect to matters within the province of proper investigation. This, of course, assumes that the constitutional rights of witnesses will be respected by the Congress as they are in a court of justice. The Bill of Rights is applicable to investigations as to all forms of governmental action. Witnesses cannot be compelled to give evidence against themselves. They cannot be subjected to unreasonable search and seizure. Nor can the First Amendment freedoms of speech, press, religion, or political belief and association be abridged.

The rudiments of the power to punish for "contempt of Congress" come to us from the pages of English history. . . .

Modern times have seen a remarkable restraint in the

use by Parliament of its contempt power. Important investigations, like those conducted in America by congressional committees, are made by Royal Commissions of Inquiry. These commissions are comprised of experts in the problem to be studied. They are removed from the turbulent forces of politics and partisan considerations. Seldom, if ever, have these commissions been given authority to compel the testimony of witnesses or the production of documents. Their success in fulfilling their fact-finding missions without resort to coercive tactics is a tribute to the fairness of the processes to the witnesses and their close adherence to the subject matter committed to them.

The history of contempt of the legislature in this country is notably different from that of England. In the early days of the United States, there lingered the direct knowledge of the evil effects of absolute power. Most of the instances of use of compulsory process by the first Congresses concerned matters affecting the qualification or integrity of their members or came about in inquiries dealing with suspected corruption or mismanagement of government officials. Unlike the English practice, from the very outset the use of contempt power by the legislature was deemed subject to judicial review.

There was very little use of the power of compulsory process in early years to enable the Congress to obtain facts pertinent to the enactment of new statutes or the administration of existing laws. The first occasion for such an investigation arose in 1827 when the House of Representatives was considering a revision of the tariff laws. In the Senate, there was no use of a fact-finding investigation in aid of legislation until 1859. In the Legislative Reorganization Act, the Committee on Un-American Activities is the only standing committee of the House of Representatives that was given the power to compel disclosures.

It is not surprising, from the fact that the House of Congress so sparingly employed the power to conduct investigations, that there have been few cases requiring judicial review of the power. The nation was almost one hundred years old before the first case reached this Court to challenge the use of compulsory process as a legislative device, rather than in inquiries concerning the elections or privileges of Congressmen. In *Kilbourn v. Thompson,* 103 U.S. 168, decided in 1881, an investigation had been authorized by the House of Representatives to learn the circumstances surrounding the bankruptcy of Jay Cooke & Company, in which the United States had deposited funds. The committee became particularly interested in a private real estate pool that was a part of the financial structure. The Court found that the subject matter of the inquiry was "in its nature clearly judicial and therefore one in respect to which no valid legislation could be enacted." The House had thereby exceeded the limits of its own authority.

Subsequent to the decision in *Kilbourn,* until recent times, there were very few cases dealing with the investigative power. The matter came to the fore again when the Senate undertook to study the corruption in handling of oil leases in the 1920's. In *McGrain v. Daugherty,* 273 U.S. 135, and *Sinclair v. United States,* 279 U.S. 263, the Court applied the precepts of *Kilbourn* to uphold the authority of the Congress to conduct the challenged investigations. The Court recognized the danger to effective and honest conduct of the Government if the legislature's power to probe corruption in the executive branch were unduly hampered.

Following these important decisions, there was another lull in judicial review of investigations. The absence of challenge, however, was not indicative of the absence of inquiries. To the contrary, there was vigorous use of the investigative power by a Congress bent upon harnessing and directing the vast economic and social forces of the times. Only one case came before this Court, and the authority of the Congress was affirmed.

In the decade following World War II, there appeared a new kind of congressional inquiry unknown in prior periods of American history. Principally this was the result of the various investigations into the threat of subversion of the United States Government, but other subjects of congressional interest also contributed to the changed scene. This new phase of legislative inquiry involved a broad-scale intrusion into the lives and affairs of private citizens. It brought before the courts novel questions of the appropriate limits of congressional inquiry. Prior cases, like *Kilbourn, McGrain* and *Sinclair,* had defined the scope of investigative power in terms of the inherent limitations of the sources of that power. In the more recent cases, the emphasis shifted to problems of accommodating the interest of the Government with the rights and privileges of individuals. The central scheme was the application of the Bill of Rights as a restraint upon the assertion of governmental power in this form.

It was during this period that the Fifth Amendment privilege against self-incrimination was frequently invoked and recognized as a legal limit upon the authority of a committee to require that a witness answer its questions. Some early doubts as to the applicability of that privilege before a legislative committee never matured. When the matter reached this Court, the Government did not challenge in any way that the Fifth Amendment protection was available to the witness, and such a challenge could not have prevailed. It confined its argument to the character of the answers sought and to the adequacy of the claim of privilege. . . .

A far more difficult task evolved from the claim by witnesses that the committees' interrogations were infringements upon the freedoms of the First Amendment. Clearly, an investigation is subject to the command that the Congress shall make no law abridging freedom of speech or press or assembly. While it is true that there is no statute to be reviewed, and that an investigation is not a law, nevertheless an investigation is part of lawmaking. It is justified solely as an adjunct to the legislative process. The First Amendment may be invoked against infringement of the protected freedoms by law or by lawmaking.

Abuses of the investigative process may imperceptibly lead to abridgment of protected freedoms. The mere summoning of a witness and compelling him to testify, against his will, about his beliefs, expressions or associations is a measure of governmental interference. And when those forced revelations concern matters that are unorthodox, unpopular, or even hateful to the general public, the reaction in the life of the witness may be disastrous. This effect is even more harsh when it is past beliefs, expressions or associations that are disclosed and judged by current standards rather than those contemporary with the matters exposed. Nor does the witness alone suffer the consequences. Those who are identified by witnesses and thereby placed in the same glare of publicity are equally subject to public stigma, scorn and obloquy. Beyond that, there is the more subtle and immeasurable effect upon those who tend to adhere to the most orthodox and uncontroversial views and associations in order to avoid a similar fate at some future time. That this impact is partly the result of non-governmental activity by private persons cannot relieve the investigators of their responsibility for initiating the reaction.

The Court recognized the restraints of the Bill of Rights upon congressional investigations in *United States v. Rumely,* 345 U.S. 41. The magnitude and complexity of the problem of applying the First Amendment to that case led the Court to construe narrowly the resolution describing the committee's authority. It was concluded that, when the First Amendment rights are threatened, the delegation of power to the committee must be clearly revealed in its charter.

Accommodation of the congressional need for particular information with the individual and personal interest in privacy is an arduous and delicate task for any court. We do not underestimate the difficulties that would attend such an undertaking. It is manifest that despite the adverse effects which follow upon compelled disclosure of private matters, not all such inquires are barred. *Kilbourn v. Thompson* teaches that such an investigation into individual affairs is invalid if unrelated to any legislative purpose. That is beyond the powers conferred upon the Congress in the Constitution. *United States v. Rumely* makes it plain that the mere semblance of legislative purpose would not justify an inquiry in the face of the Bill of Rights. The critical element is the existence of, and the weight to be ascribed to, the interest of the Congress in demanding disclosures from an unwilling witness. We cannot simply assume, however, that every congressional investigation is justified by a public need that overbalances any private rights affected. To do so would be to abdicate the responsibility placed by the Constitution upon the judiciary to insure that the Congress does not unjustifiably encroach upon an individual's right to privacy nor abridge his liberty of speech, press, religion or assembly.

Petitioner has earnestly suggested that the difficult questions of protecting these rights from infringement by legislative inquiries can be surmounted in this case because there was no public purpose served in his interrogation. His conclusion is based upon the thesis that the Subcommittee was engaged in a program of exposure for the sake of exposure. The sole purpose of the inquiry, he contends, was to bring down upon himself and others the violence of public reaction because of their past beliefs, expressions and associations. In support of this argument, petitioner has marshalled an impressive array of evidence that some Congressmen have believed that such was their duty, or part of it.

We have no doubt that there is no congressional power to expose for the sake of exposure. The public is, of course, entitled to be informed concerning the workings of its government. That cannot be inflated into a general power to expose where the predominant result can only be an invasion of the private rights of individuals. But a solution to our problem is not to be found in testing the motives of committee members for this purpose. Such is not our function. Their motives alone would not vitiate an investigation which had been instituted by a House of Congress if that assembly's legislative purpose is being served.

Petitioner's contentions do point to a situation of particular significance from the standpoint of the constitutional limitations upon congressional investigations. The theory of a committee inquiry is that the committee members are serving as the representatives of the parent assembly in collecting information for a legislative purpose. Their function is to act as the eyes and ears of the Congress in obtaining facts upon which the full legislature can act. To carry out this mission, committees and subcommittees, sometimes one Congressman, are endowed with the full power of the Congress to compel testimony. In this case, only two men exercised that authority in demanding information over petitioner's protest.

An essential premise in this situation is that the House or Senate shall have instructed the committee members on what they are to do with the power delegated to them. It is the responsibility of the Congress, in the first instance, to insure that compulsory process is used only in furtherance of a legislative purpose. That requires that the instructions to an investigating committee spell out that group's jurisdiction and purpose with sufficient particularity. Those instructions are embodied in the authorizing resolution. That document is the committee's charter. Broadly drafted and loosely worded, however, such resolutions can leave tremendous latitude to the discretion of the investigators. The more vague the committee's charter is, the greater becomes the possibility that the committee's specific actions are not in conformity with the will of the parent House of Congress.

The authorizing resolution of the Un-American Activities Committee was adopted in 1938 when a select committee, under the chairmanship of Representative Dies, was created. Several years later, the Committee was made a standing organ of the House with the same mandate. It defines the Committee's authority as follows:

> "The Committee on Un-American Activities, as a whole or by subcommittee, is authorized to make from time to time investigations of (i) the extent, character, and objects of un-American propaganda activities in the United States, (ii) the diffusion within the United States of subversive and un-American propaganda that is instigated from foreign countries or of a domestic origin and attacks the principle of the form of government as guaranteed by our Constitution, and (iii) all other questions in relation thereto that would aid Congress in any necessary remedial legislation."

It would be difficult to imagine a less explicit authorizing resolution. Who can define the meaning of "un-American"? What is that single, solitary "principle of the form of government as guaranteed by our Constitution"? There is no need to dwell upon the language, however. At one time, perhaps, the resolution might have been read narrowly to confine the Committee to the subject of propaganda. The events that have transpired in the fifteen years before the interrogation of petitioner make such a construction impossible at this date. The members of the Committee have clearly demonstrated that they did not feel themselves restricted in any way to propaganda in the narrow sense of the word. Unquestionably the Committee conceived of its task in the grand view of its name. Un-American activities were its target, no matter how or where manifested. Notwithstanding the broad purview of the Committee's experience, the House of Representatives repeatedly approved its continuation. Five times it extended the life of the special committee. Then it made the group a standing committee of the House. A year later, the Committee's charter was embodied in the Legislative Reorganization Act. On five occasions, at the beginning of sessions of Congress, it has made the authorizing resolution part of the rules of the House. On innumerable occasions, it has passed appropriation bills to allow the Committee to continue its efforts.

Combining the language of the resolution with the construction it has been given, it is evident that the preliminary control of the Committee exercised by the House of Representatives is slight or non-existent. No one could reasonably deduce from the charter the kind of investigation that the Committee was directed to make. As a result, we are asked to engage in a process of retroactive rationalization. Looking backward from the events that transpired, we are asked to uphold the Committee's actions unless it appears that they were clearly not authorized by the charter. As a corollary to this inverse approach, the Government urges that we must view the matter hospitably to the power of the Congress—that if there is any legislative power which might have been furthered by the kind of disclosure sought, the witness must be punished for withholding it. No doubt every reasonable indulgence of legality must be accorded to the actions of a coordinate branch of our Government. But such deference cannot yield to an unnecessary and unreasonable dissipation of precious constitutional freedoms.

The Government contends that the public interest at the core of the investigations of the Un-American Activities Committee is the need by the Congress to be informed of efforts to overthrow the Government by force and violence so that adequate legislative safeguards can be erected. From this core, however, the Committee can radiate outward infinitely to any topic thought to be related in some way to armed insurrection. The outer reaches of this domain are known only by the content of "un-American activities." Remoteness of subject can be aggravated by a probe for a depth of detail even farther removed from any basis of legislative action. A third dimension is added when the investigators turn their attention to the past to collect minutiae on remote topics, on the hypothesis that the past may reflect upon the present.

The consequences that flow from this situation are manifold. In the first place, a reviewing court is unable to make the kind of judgment made by the Court in *United States v. Rumely, supra.* The Committee is allowed, in essence, to define its own authority, to choose the direction and focus of its activities. In deciding what to do with the power that has been conferred upon them, members of the Committee may act pursuant to motives that seem to them to be the highest. Their decisions, nevertheless, can lead to ruthless exposure of private lives in order to gather data that is neither desired by the Congress nor useful to it. Yet it is impossible in this circumstance, with constitutional freedoms in jeopardy, to declare that the Committee has ranged beyond the area committed to it by its parent assembly because the boundaries are so nebulous.

More important and more fundamental than that, however, it insulates the House that has authorized the investigation from the witnesses who are subjected to the sanctions of compulsory process. There is a wide gulf between the responsibility for the use of investigative power and the actual exercise of that power. This is an especially vital consideration in assuring respect for constitutional liberties. Protected freedoms should not be placed in danger in the absence of a clear determination by the House or the Senate that a particular inquiry is justified by a specific legislative need.

It is, of course, not the function of this Court to prescribe rigid rules for the Congress to follow in drafting resolutions establishing investigating committees. That is a matter peculiarly within the realm of the legislature, and its decisions will be accepted by the courts up to the point where their own duty to enforce the constitutionally protected rights of individuals is affected. An excessively broad charter, like that of the House Un-American Activities Committee, places the courts in an untenable position if they are to strike a balance between the public need for a particular interrogation and the right of citizens to carry on their affairs free from unnecessary governmental interference. It is impossible in such a situation to ascertain whether any legislative purpose justifies the disclosure sought and, if so, the importance of that information to the Congress in furtherance of its legislative function. The reason no court can make this critical judgment is that the House of Representatives itself has never made it. Only the legislative assembly initiating an investigation can assay the relative necessity of specific disclosures.

Absence of the qualitative consideration of petitioner's questioning by the House of Representatives aggravates a serious problem, revealed in this case, in the relationship of congressional investigating committees and the witnesses who appear before them. Plainly these committees are restricted to the missions delegated to them, *i.e.*, to acquire certain data to be used by the House or the Senate in coping with a problem that falls within its legislative sphere. No witness can be compelled to make disclosures on matters outside that area. This is a jurisdictional concept of pertinency drawn from the nature of a congressional committee's source of authority. It is not wholly different from nor unrelated to the elements of pertinency embodied in the criminal statute under which petitioner was prosecuted. When the definition of jurisdictional pertinency is as uncertain and wavering as in the case of the Un-American Activities Committee, it becomes extremely difficult for the Committee to limit its inquiries to statutory pertinency.

Since World War II, the Congress has practically abandoned its original practice of utilizing the coercive sanction of contempt proceedings at the bar of the House. The sanction there imposed is imprisonment by the House until the recalcitrant witness agrees to testify or disclose the matters sought, provided that the incarceration does not extend beyond adjournment. The Congress has instead invoked the aid of the federal judicial system in protecting itself against contumacious conduct. It has become customary to refer these matters to the United States

Attorneys for prosecution under criminal law.

The appropriate statute is found in 2 U.S.C. section 192. It provides:

> "Every person who having been summoned as a witness by the authority of either House of Congress to give testimony or to produce papers upon any matter under inquiry before either House, or any joint committee established by a joint or concurrent resolution of the two Houses of Congress, or any committee of either House of Congress, willfully makes default, or who, having appeared, refuses to answer any question pertinent to the question under inquiry, shall be deemed guilty of a misdemeanor, punishable by a fine of not more than $1,000 nor less than $100 and imprisonment in a common jail for not less than one month nor more than twelve months."

In fulfillment of their obligation under this statute, the courts must accord to the defendants every right which is guaranteed to defendants in all other criminal cases. Among these is the right to have available, through a sufficiently precise statute, information revealing the standard of criminality before the commission of the alleged offense. Applied to persons prosecuted under section 192, this raises a special problem in that the statute defines the crime as refusal to answer "any question pertinent to the question under inquiry." Part of the standard of criminality, therefore, is the pertinency of the questions propounded to the witness.

The problem attains proportion when viewed from the standpoint of the witness who appears before a congressional committee. He must decide at the time the questions are propounded whether or not to answer. As the Court said in *Sinclair v. United States*, 279 U.S. 263, the witness acts at his peril. He is ". . . bound rightly to construe the statute." *Id.*, at 299. An erroneous determination on his part, even if made in the utmost good faith, does not exculpate him if the court should later rule that the questions were pertinent to the question under inquiry.

It is obvious that a person compelled to make this choice is entitled to have knowledge of the subject to which the interrogation is deemed pertinent. That knowledge must be available with the same degree of explicitness and clarity that the Due Process Clause requires in the expression of any element of a criminal offense. The "vice of vagueness" must be avoided here as in all other crimes. There are several sources that can outline the "question under inquiry" in such a way that the rules against vagueness are satisfied. The authorizing resolution, the remarks of the chairman or members of the committee, or even the nature of the proceedings themselves might sometimes make the topic clear. This case demonstrates, however, that these sources often leave the matter in grave doubt.

That issue is not before us, however, in light of the Government's position that the immediate subject under inquiry before the Subcommittee interviewing petitioner was only one aspect of the Committee's authority to investigate un-American activities. Distilling that single topic from the broad field is an extremely difficult task upon the record before us. There was an opening statement by the Committee Chairman at the outset of the hearing, but this gives us no guidance. In this statement, the Chairman did no more than paraphrase the authorizing resolution and give a very general sketch of the past efforts of the Committee.

No aid is given as to the "question under inquiry" in the action of the full Committee that authorized the creation of the Subcommittee before which petitioner appeared. The Committee adopted a formal resolution giving the Chairman the power to appoint subcommittees ". . . for the purpose of performing any and all acts which the Committee as a whole is authorized to do." In effect, this was a device to enable the investigations to proceed with a quorum of one or two members and sheds no light on the relevancy of the questions asked of petitioner.

The Government believes that the topic of inquiry before the Subcommittee concerned Communist infiltration in labor. In his introductory remarks, the Chairman made reference to a bill, then pending before the Committee, which would have penalized labor unions controlled or dominated by persons who were, or had been, members of a "Communist-action" organization, as defined in the Internal Security Act of 1950. The Subcommittee, it is contended, might have been endeavoring to determine the extent of such a problem.

This view is corroborated somewhat by the witnesses who preceded and followed petitioner before the Subcommittee. Looking at the entire hearings, however, there is strong reason to doubt that the subject revolved about labor matters. The published transcript is entitled: Investigation of Communist Activities in the Chicago Area, and six of the nine witnesses had no connection with labor at all.

The most serious doubts as to the Subcommittee's "question under inquiry," however, stem from the precise questions that petitioner has been charged with refusing to answer. Under the terms of the statute, after all, it is these which must be proved pertinent. Petitioner is charged with refusing to tell the Subcommittee whether or not he knew that certain named persons had been members of the Communist Party in the past. The Subcommittee's counsel read the list from the testimony of a previous witness who had identified them as Communists. Although this former witness was identified with labor, he had not stated that the persons he named were involved in union affairs. Of the thirty names propounded to petitioner, seven were completely unconnected with organized labor. One operated a beauty parlor. Another was a watchmaker. Several were identified as "just citizens" or "only Communists." When almost a quarter of the persons on the list are not labor people, the inference becomes strong that the subject before the Subcommittee was not defined in terms of Communism in labor.

The final source of evidence as to the "question under inquiry" is the Chairman's response when petitioner objected to the questions on the ground of lack of pertinency. The Chairman then announced that the Subcommittee was investigating "subversion and subversive propaganda." This is a subject at least as broad and indefinite as the authorizing resolution of the Committee, if not more so.

Having exhausted the several possible indicia of the "question under inquiry," we remain unenlightened as to the subject to which the questions asked petitioner were pertinent. Certainly, if the point is that obscure after trial and appeal, it was not adequately revealed to petitioner when he had to decide at his peril whether or not to answer. Fundamental fairness demands that no witness be compelled to make such a determination with so little guidance. Unless the subject matter has been made to appear with undisputable clarity, it is the duty of the investigative body, upon objection of the witness on grounds of pertinency, to state for the record the subject under inquiry at that time and the manner in which the propounded questions are pertinent thereto. To be meaningful, the explanation must describe what the topic under inquiry is and the connective reasoning whereby the precise questions asked relate to it.

The statement of the Committee Chairman in this case, in response to petitioner's protest, was woefully inadequate to convey sufficient information as to the pertinency of the questions to the subject under inquiry. Petitioner was thus not accorded a fair opportunity to determine whether he was within his rights in refusing to answer, and his conviction is necessarily invalid under the Due Process Clause of the Fifth Amendment.

We are mindful of the complexities of modern government and the ample scope that must be left to the Congress as the sole constitutional depository of legislative power. Equally mindful are we of the indispensable function, in the exercise of that power, of congressional investigations. The conclusions we have reached in this case will not prevent the Congress, through its committees, from obtaining any information it needs for the proper fulfillment of its role in our scheme of government. The legislature is free to determine the kinds of data that should be collected. It is only those investigations that are conducted by use of compulsory process that give rise to a need to protect the rights of individuals against illegal encroachment. That protection can be readily achieved through procedures which prevent the separation of power from responsibility and which provide the constitutional requisites of fairness for witnesses. A measure of added care on the part of the House and the Senate in authorizing the use of compulsory process and by their committees in exercising that power would suffice. That is a small price to pay if it serves to uphold the principles of limited constitutional government without constricting the power of the Congress to inform itself.

INDEX

VAN NOSTRAND ANVIL BOOKS already published